Freedom Within Reason

Freedom
Within Reason

Susan Wolf

New York   Oxford
OXFORD UNIVERSITY PRESS
1990

Oxford University Press

Oxford   New York   Toronto
Delhi   Bombay   Calcutta   Madras   Karachi
Petaling Jaya   Singapore   Hong Kong   Tokyo
Nairobi   Dar es Salaam   Cape Town
Melbourne   Auckland

and associated companies in
Berlin   Ibadan

Published by Oxford University Press, Inc.,
200 Madison Avenue, New York, NY 10016

Oxford is a registered trademark of Oxford University Press

Library of Congress Cataloging-in-Publication Data
Wolf, Susan R.
Freedom within reason/ by Susan Wolf.
p.   cm.   Includes bibliographical references.
ISBN 0-19-505616-7
1. Free will and determinism.   2. Ethics.   3. Reason.   I. Title.
BJ1461.W64   1990   123'.5—dc20   89-77306

1 3 5 7 9 8 6 4 2

Printed in the United States of America
on acid-free paper

To my parents, Ludwig and Hilde Wolf

Preface

Free will is arguably the most difficult problem in philosophy. Given the centuries of thought, even of deep and brilliant thought, that have been devoted to this problem, it would not be unreasonable to assume that only fools rush in, at this point, thinking they have something to say about it. Yet I do think I have something to say about it. Readers will undoubtedly draw their own conclusions.

Whether or not free will is one of the most difficult problems, it is certainly one of the most gripping. Reflections on religion, psychology, physics, education, and on the issue of crime and punishment all lead to the problems of free will and responsibility, and one has only to read Dostoevsky to get a sense of the urgency with which these problems may be felt. These problems are neither invented by nor restricted to academic philosphers. To the contrary, they testify to a philosophical urge in human nature. This book is addressed to all those whose philosophical urge expresses itself in a concern with free will.

This book is not the most comprehensive presentation and defense of the views within it that could be written. I submit the book not just with the abstract knowledge that it contains mistakes (what book doesn't?) but with the concrete and painful awareness of ways it might be revised that would perhaps present and defend my ideas more successfully. But to quote Mick Jagger, "I have my freedom, but I don't have much time." Obviously, I must accept full responsibility for whatever errors and flaws this book contains.

The book neither addresses nor acknowledges much of the important historical and contemporary literature on the subject. In part, my writing a book of this sort rather than one that engages more directly with the relevant literature is a matter of choice: I wanted to write an uncluttered book that formulates and addresses problems in the ways I have found to be most natural and beneficial and that will appeal and be accessible to nonspecialists as well as specialists. In part, however, the form of the book is also a consequence of my philosophical personality: My own involvement with the problems examined here (and an impatient nature) made it difficult for me to attend responsibly to the writings of others while I was still trying to formulate my own thoughts on the subject. I hope that, with this initial formulation completed, I will be able to be more attentive to the questions, problems, and insights contained in the voluminous literature on free will and to address some of the issues it raises in other contexts.

Although this book touches on subjects that are potentially of great practical importance (for example, criminal punishment, insanity, and moral education), it offers little that can be put directly to practical use. If anything, accepting the book's claims only highlights the difficulties of settling these matters with confidence. It would be a great benefit of a theory of responsibility if it gave one substantive help in determining whether and how much individuals are responsible for specific concrete actions. But this benefit would not be a reason for believing that theory, and the lack of it does not provide a reason for rejecting one. My views, at least, offer a conception of what kinds of work need to be done and what kinds of questions need to be answered if we are to improve our ability to make judgments of such practical significance.

My interest in the problems of free will and responsibility is as old as, perhaps older than, my interest in academic philosophy, and the development of the ideas expressed in this book began before I finished graduate school. As a result, it is tempting to acknowledge everyone who has contributed to my philosophical work in general, as well as to this book in particular. But I have had so much help—from teachers and colleagues at Yale, Princeton, Harvard, the University of Maryland, Dartmouth, and Johns Hopkins, as well as from many others who have corresponded and talked with me in other professional contexts—that an attempt to name them all would inevitably fall short. Jonathan Bennett, John Martin Fischer, Derek Parfit, Mark Ravizza, Thomas Scanlon, Ferdinand Schoeman, Judith Jarvis Thomson, and Gary Watson deserve special mention for their discussions of parts of the manuscript or related works, from which I have especially benefited. I also owe thanks to Camille Smith for valuable editorial assistance.

Portions of this work have been supported by fellowships from the American Council of Learned Societies, the American Association of University Women, and the University of Maryland Research Board. I am deeply grateful to them.

P. F. Strawson's "Freedom and Resentment" and Iris Murdoch's *The Sovereignty of Good* were immeasurably important in focusing my interest in and shaping the views on freedom and responsibility that are developed here.

Douglas MacLean, with whom I have discussed these issues from the very beginning of my thinking about them, has provided invaluable criticism, advice, encouragement, not to mention emotional and material sustenance, throughout.

My greatest debt in this work is to Thomas Nagel, whose inspiration, criticism, and encouragement made this book possible, and whose commitment to clarity and depth and to truth and passion in philosophy has given me the standard toward which I aspire.

Baltimore, Md.   S. W.
January 1990

Contents

Freedom Within Reason

1

The Dilemma of Autonomy

(In Which the Problems of Responsibility and Free Will Are Presented)

To be accorded the status of a responsible being is to be regarded as an appropriate object of a certain range of attitudes and judgments and as a legitimate participant in a certain range of practices. The range of attitudes I have in mind includes pride and shame, gratitude and resentment, respect and contempt. The range of judgments includes the judgment that one is worthy of respect or contempt, that one ought to be proud or ashamed, and so on. And the range of practices includes praising and blaming, forgiving, excusing, rewarding, and punishing according to rules designed to make these practices expressions of the above sorts of attitudes and judgments.

It is a deep and essential feature of life in modern Western society that normal human beings who have reached some level of maturity regard themselves and one another as responsible beings. That is, if people did not regard themselves and one another as responsible beings, life would be unrecognizably different from what it actually is. But the concept of responsibility is a mysterious one which tends, on examination, to become increasingly opaque and to threaten variously to be incoherent or impossible or universally inapplicable. Thus there is a philosophical problem of responsibility and, connected to it, a philosophical problem of free will, understanding free

3

will to be that relation to one's will which is necessary in order for one's actions (as well as one's character and life insofar as they are governable by one's will) to be "up to oneself" in the way that is necessary for responsibility. We can express the problem of responsibility in the form of the question "How, if at all, is responsibility possible?" And we can express the problem of free will in the form of the question "What must our relation to our wills be," or better, perhaps, "What kind of beings must *we* be if we are ever to be responsible for the results of our wills?"

This book is unabashedly devoted to solving these problems, though to put it that way suggests an incredible *hubris* on the part of the author, and might also mislead the reader into thinking that the book is intended to put these problems, once and for all, to rest. It would be just as accurate to describe the book's aim as to provide a way of understanding—or, if you like, interpeting—these problems. In other words, this book is an attempt to put these problems in a new light, a light that shows their connections to other problems and that directs our way of thinking about them along paths that have long been unexplored.

But the very existence of problems that can be expressed in the form of the questions above is not self-evident. These questions may appear to be alternatively trivial or unintelligible. For the troublesome sense of mystery or opacity that attaches to the concept of responsibility is not a universal or a natural affliction. In the absence of intrusive philosophical thought, we are comfortable with the attitudes and practices associated with responsibility and with the patterns of thought by which these attitudes and practices are formed, defended, and withdrawn. To the question "How, if at all, is responsibility possible?" one might be inclined to reply "Why shouldn't it be possible?" And to the question "What kinds of beings must we be if we are ever to be responsible for the results of our wills?" one might be inclined to answer "Why, we must be precisely the kinds of beings that we are!"

Setting Up the Problem(s): The Dilemma of Autonomy

The acquisition of tendencies to take the attitudes, form the judgments, engage in the practices that are associated with responsibility, and to do so in accordance with the relevant patterns of thought, occurs, for members of contemporary Western culture, as a part of our natural development. These tendencies arise as part and parcel of the enlargement and enrichment of our consciousness of the world and of our repertoire of responses to it that constitute our growth from psychological infancy to psychological maturity. As the sense of well-being and its opposite and the feelings of pleasure and displeasure associated with distinct individuals and objects that we experience as infants are gradually differentiated into kinds, we begin to have identifiable feelings of pride, shame, and guilt, to feel admiration for (some) others, to be vulnerable to having our feelings hurt, to feel gratitude, resentment, and eventually respect, contempt, and indignation. As we develop these feelings and attitudes, we learn to discriminate between occasions in which these feelings and attitudes are and are not appropriate. We learn to feel pride and shame about some aspects of ourselves but not others, to feel gratitude and resentment toward some individuals but not others, and to have these feelings on the basis of some but not other features and actions of the relevant individuals. In conjunction with the expansion of our range of attitudes and feelings and the increase in our ability to direct them, there is an increasing tendency on the part of others to take the attitudes associated with responsibility toward us, and to regard us as appropriate objects of these attitudes. Thus, the development of our tendencies to form such attitudes toward ourselves and others is at one with the development of distinctive kinds of relationships and forms of interaction with the individuals toward whom we take these attitudes and who take these attitudes toward us.

In this way, we acquire senses of ourselves and (some) others as responsible beings, as beings with a distinctive kind of status in the world, whose relations to each other and to the world at large are different in kind from the relations that nonresponsible beings are capable of forming and having. Although it is notoriously difficult to say in what, precisely, this distinctiveness consists, certain kinds of imagery and modes of expression seem peculiarly apt in our attempts to elaborate it—the imagery of depth and power, and the tendency to put the difference between responsible and nonresponsible beings in terms that suggest that the former have a special kind of significance. We take responsible beings more seriously than we take nonresponsible ones—we treat them as persons, and not as objects. We credit them and hold them to blame for things in a way that suggests that we attribute events and qualities to them more deeply than we do to others. These beings seem to have a special kind of power or control over what they do and who they are, in virtue of which they are owed a special attitude of respect and are endowed with a special kind of value.

It seems natural and reasonable for us generally to grant ourselves and creatures relevantly like us the status of responsibility and not to grant this status to beings who differ from us in salient ways. Moreover, it seems natural and reasonable for us to distinguish aspects of our behavior and personality for which we apparently are responsible from those for which we apparently are not. By examining the patterns of our attributions of responsibility, we are able to formulate conditions of responsibility, features of an agent and of her relation to some event, object, or property that are required if the attitudes and judgments connected to responsibility are to be deemed appropriate and justifiable. For example, it seems necessary that an agent be capable of having thoughts of a certain kind and that she be able to govern her behavior in light of these thoughts, and it seems necessary that the agent's behavior be free of certain constraints or interferences that may be imposed by drugs or hypnosis or deception. But when our examination goes beyond the mere cataloguing of the diverse and relatively specific conditions of responsibility that we are apt to invoke to explain our responses to agents and events in concrete situations, when we try to find more general features in our patterns of attributing responsibility that will explain and organize these specific conditions in a systematic or enlightening way, the concept of responsibility begins to seem problematic. For the attempt to understand why the specific and diverse conditions of responsibility *are* conditions of responsibility can lead us to formulate a more general condition, to which all these more specific ones may be understood to point, which casts doubt upon the appropriateness of our attributions of responsibility even in what formerly seemed to be our most central cases.[1] In other words, we can be led to believe that there is a condition of responsibility that it is doubtful any of us ever satisfy, a condition that may seem impossible to satisfy and that may imply that the concept of responsibility is incoherent.

This is one route that may lead us to ask the question "How, if at all, is responsibility possible?" A positive answer to this question would then seem to have to take one of two possible forms: Either it would show us that the apparently impossible condition of responsibility is not a condition of responsibility after all, or it would show us that this apparently impossible condition is one that it is possible, even plausible, to think we regularly satisfy.

Let us see what this apparently impossible condition is, and what considerations might lead us to accept it. It is obvious enough that one condition of responsibility involves the possession of a will. In other words, only an agent who has a will—that is, who has desires, goals, or purposes and the ability to control her behavior in accordance with them—can be responsible for anything at all. A volcanic mountain is not responsible for erupting, a defective tire is not responsible for skidding, because these objects, and inanimate objects generally, cannot be said to have control over their characteristics or behavior. Unlike agents that have wills, these individuals, if they can be said to be agents at all, cannot direct their own actions or choose what effects they will produce. Moreover, an agent that has a will can be responsible only for things that are related to her in such a way that they fall, so to speak, within the sphere of influence of her will. Thus an agent is not responsible for the color of her eyes or her susceptibility to sunburn. She is not responsible for her silence if she has been gagged or for her handprints on a wall into which she has been pushed. More generally, an agent can be responsible only for events and properties that stand in a relation to her such that her will is or could have been *effective* in determining the existence of these events or properties.

But clearly the possession of a potentially effective will is not enough to warrant attributions of responsibility. Dogs and cats, young children, the insane, and severely mentally retarded adults have potentially effective wills, and yet we do not regard them as responsible beings. Though these individuals have a kind of control of their behavior, they cannot control their behavior along the right lines. That is, they cannot control their behavior with respect to the features that would be relevant to judgments of responsibility. One would not, for example, blame the neighbor's dog for eating the brownies one baked for a picnic in the way in which one might blame a housemate for doing the same thing. One would not credit a child who, in playing with fingerpaints, produced a beautiful picture in the same way that one would credit a more mature artist who produced an equally beautiful painting. When we judge an agent responsible for some event (or object or character trait), our judgment is made against a background of imagined alternatives that could have but did not occur and against a background of reasons that did or could have influenced the agent in question to do one thing rather than another. When we judge an agent responsible for some event (or object or character trait), we might say, we judge her responsible for that event under a certain description, with some feature or features more or less distinctly in mind that give that event its positive, neutral, or negative value. In order for an agent to be responsible for an event or object or character trait, the agent's will must be not only potentially effective in determining the event's occurrence or the object or trait's existence but also, as it were, potentially intelligent: That is, it must be possible for the features that might weigh in favor of or against that event in relevant ways to enter into the determination or the content of the agent's will. We do not regard the dog or the child in the examples above as responsible for their actions because the dog and the child could not possibly be influenced by the relevant moral or aesthetic considerations. Whole classes of beings may be generically excluded from the set of individuals who might deserve the status of responsibility if they lack basic intellectual capacities that are necessary for the possession of a suitably intelligent will. In addition, individuals who are generally capable of comprehending the relevant sorts of features may be exempt from responsibility for particular actions if, owing to unavoidable ignorance or inexperience, for example, they are incapable of recognizing features that are relevant to a particular situation on a particular occasion.

It is a condition of responsibility, then, that an agent possess a potentially effective and relevantly intelligent will (that is, a will whose content can be informed and governed by the relevant considerations). This condition accounts for many of our intuitions concerning the appropriate attributions of responsibility in a way that coheres with the meaning responsibility and the attitudes connected to it have for us. It makes sense that we should take agents who can control their behavior in intelligent ways more seriously than other agents; it makes sense that we should regard the features of the world that fall within the sphere of their intelligent control as being more deeply attributable to them; and it makes sense that we should regard these features as saying more about them, as being deeper or more significant indications of these agent's selves.

A further survey of our patterns of attribution of responsibility, however, suggests that the condition formulated above is still not a sufficient condition of responsibility. We can easily imagine cases of individuals who have potentially effective and relevantly intelligent wills but who nonetheless do not seem responsible for the actions that are a result of their wills. A person who, under hypnosis, has been instructed to obey the commands of her hypnotizer without question, may be subsequently told by her hypnotizer to treat a third person with the utmost kindness and consideration. When the hypnotized agent obeys, she must utilize her ability to recognize kindness and consideration in shaping her behavior. But though she acts kindly and considerately on purpose, she does not deserve the gratitude of the beneficiary of her acts. A person, threatened with violence to himself or others who are dear to him, may betray a confidence fully aware of the considerations that weigh against his act. He acts intentionally and knows what he is doing, but, if the threat is serious enough, he is not blameworthy for his action. Finally, a kleptomaniac who steals a piece of jewelry from a store intentionally performs an action she knows to be criminal and wrong. Indeed, the fact that her action has these properties may be essential to her motivation to perform it. Yet she is not responsible for stealing—the action is not deeply attributable to her.

At one level, the explanations for why the agents in these examples are not responsible for their actions appear quite diverse and unrelated. In the hypnosis example, we might focus on the fact that although the agent acts on a desire *in* her—a desire to act kindly and considerately—there is a sense in which the desire is not "really" hers; it has been implanted in her by the hypnotist. The motivating desire of the man in the coercion example, however— the desire to protect himself or a loved one from harm—is not a desire that in ordinary circumstances would cast doubt on the man's responsibility. Here the problem lies in the imposition of a situation that manipulates the agent by means of his desires. The situation is such that given the agent's desires, which may be unobjectionable in themselves, the agent cannot help acting on these desires in a particular way. The case of the kleptomaniac differs from the others in not involving external manipulation at all. Yet like the hypnotized woman, the kleptomaniac seems to have a desire she cannot help having, and like the coerced man, the kleptomaniac seems compelled to act on her desire in a particular way.

The agents in these cases are not responsible for their actions despite the fact that their wills are effective and relevantly informed. The agents act intentionally and in light of the features of their actions that make those actions alternatively good or bad. Although at one level the explanations for why these various agents are nonetheless exempt from responsibility may appear diverse, at another level they may seem fundamentally the same. For in each case the problem is neither with the effectiveness nor with the content of the agent's will. It is rather with the source of the agent's will—with the fact that the agent is not in control of what the content of his or her will will be. The agents in these cases seem to be mere vehicles of change in the world rather than initiators of it. The control they have of their behavior seems to be only control of an intermediate kind. Though their behavior results from the content of their wills, the content of their wills results from something else, and this something else is such that the agents are powerless to choose or resist it.

It seems, then, that in addition to the requirement that the agent have control over her behavior (that she have a potentially effective will) and the requirement that she have control along the right lines (a relevantly intelligent will), there is a requirement that the agent's control be ultimate—her will must be determined by her self, and her self must not, in turn, be determined by anything external to itself. This last condition I shall call, after Kant, the requirement of autonomy.[2]

This condition, like the others, seems to cohere with the meaning responsibility has for us. It makes sense that beings who can purposefully initiate change should have a different status in the world from that of those who merely execute it. It makes sense that such beings should have a special significance, for they are sources of value (and disvalue) rather than mere carriers of it. And the imagery of depth that naturally colors our attempts to describe the difference between responsible and nonresponsible beings seems readily accounted for as an expression of the perception, however dim, that the control responsible beings exhibit is *ultimate* control. By contrast with the ultimate control of autonomous beings, the control exerted by beings whose behavior is controlled by their wills, but whose wills are controlled by something else, seems merely superficial.

At first glance, the condition of autonomy may seem no more problematic than the other conditions of responsibility. That is, it may seem to be a condition that, like the others, we satisfy most of the time. If we speak occasionally of finding ourselves with desires that are not our own, desires that move us but with which we do not or cannot identify, we do so, presumably, by contrast to a more normal state of affairs in which the desires that provide the basis for our actions are wholly and comfortably our own. And if we sometimes describe situations in which, although we act intentionally, we have no choice but to perform the actions we do, we contrast this with more typical situations in which, it seems, we do have a choice. That is, most of the time, we seem free to act in whatever way we please. We choose to do some things rather than others, and nothing makes us choose.

A closer look at ourselves and our actions, however, may make us doubt our own apparent autonomy and may suggest that the expressions that look like claims of autonomous agency are really just figures of speech. For although few of our desires are implanted in us in as obvious and unnatural a way as that in which a hypnotist implants a desire in her subject, neither do they arise out of nothing external to ourselves. My desire for a pastry is clearly a result of the smells wafting from the bakery as I walk past; my desire for a new sweater can be traced to a magazine advertisement that caught my eye. A passionate speech makes me want to write my congressman; a letter from a friend makes me want to give her a call. It seems natural that I should have these desires in these situations—they cohere with my other desires and with my general character in ways in which desires that are implanted by hypnotists may not. But the source of these desires is no less external than the source of the desires I might be hypnotized to have, and if I identify with the former but not with the latter desires, it is not because the former desires are up to me.

Similarly, it seems that, although situations are rarely imposed on us in so artificial and manipulative a way as that in which an armed criminal may coerce his victim, situations that arise in less objectionable ways push us no less firmly to act one way rather than another. Zero-degree weather makes me turn up the heat; an empty refrigerator makes me go to the store. An upcoming tenure decision makes an assistant professor write articles for publication; a child's illness makes a father leave work early to take his daughter to the doctor.

These observations suggest a picture of ourselves as creatures whose desires are a result of some combination of our heredity and environment, who try to satisfy our desires as well as we can by acting as our situations demand. But if our desires are a result of heredity and environment, they come from something external to ourselves. And if, in conjunction with our desires, the situations in which we find ourselves dictate which actions we will ultimately decide to perform, then our behavior is completely explained by forces that originate outside of ourselves. This picture seems incompatible with the satisfaction of the condition of autonomy. This condition, which we were led to accept in our effort to explain why the agents in a few exceptional cases were not responsible for their actions, now threatens to exclude all human agents in all situations from responsibility. The cases of hypnosis and coercion now seem exceptional only in being cases in which the agents' lack of autonomy is dramatically evident. But if a lack of autonomy that is dramatically evident excludes agents from responsibility, a lack of autonomy that is less easily perceived will exclude agents as well.

In light of the apparently drastic implications the conclusion that we are not autonomous beings would have, it would be foolish to accept this conclusion too easily. The remarks made above suggest that the claim that we are autonomous beings is not so obviously or so generally true as it might formerly have seemed. But they do not imply that autonomy is impossible. Perhaps the examples of "ordinary desires" and "ordinary situations" were taken from an insufficiently wide range of experiences. If we are not responsible for as large a portion of our behavior and personality as we ordinarily think, this does not imply that we are responsible for none of our actions or character at all.[3] Or, perhaps, the description of ordinary human action above is simplistic in insidious ways, omitting some elements that are crucial to a realization of autonomy.

Unfortunately, attempts to construct an alternative picture of human action, or to revise the picture presented above in a way that will justify our apparent assumption that we typically act as autonomous agents, are likely to make the condition of autonomy seem even more puzzling than before. For if the agent's control of her actions seems superficial when we add, in accordance with the picture above, that what control she exhibits is itself controlled by forces external to the agent herself, her control seems no less superficial if we remove these external forces and imagine that the agent's control is controlled by nothing at all. According to the problematic picture above, the agent's will is not wholly or deeply her own because the content of her will is completely determined by forces, people, and events external to herself. But if the content of the agent's will is not so determined—if her having the will she does is instead, in part, a result of random events, or if it is a matter of brute, inexplicable fact—this hardly seems to make her will more wholly or deeply her own. Indeed, recalling the case of the kleptomaniac, it may seem irrelevant whether the agent's will is controlled by something else or by nothing at all.

Autonomy, then, requires that the content of an agent's will (which, we may assume, determines the agent's behavior) be up to the agent herself, and this is opposed not only to its being up to anything else, but also to its not being up to anything at all. But now the concept of an autonomous agent may seem to be an impossible one. For it seems that about any agent and any act whatsoever we can ask for an explanation of why that agent performs that act. And though we may begin to answer this question in terms of features internal to the agent, we can always press beyond these beginnings and ask why the agent possesses these features. If this question in turn is answered by reference to still other features internal to the agent, we can press further and ask why the agent possesses these additional features. Eventually, we will reach a set of features that must be explained by facts external to the agent, or our explanation will simply come to an end, with the understanding that the agent's possessing these features is either a random occurrence or a brute, inexplicable fact. An agent, for example, performs some action because she wants to perform it, and she wants to perform it because she wants something else to which the action in question is perceived as a means. But why does she want that something else? Perhaps because the pursuit of that goal offers the best chance of satisfactorily realizing her complex system of values. But then we may ask why she has that particular system of values. If, on the one hand, we can answer this question by describing the agent's heredity, her upbringing, her most significant recent experiences, and so on, then the agent seems to fit the problematic model of the nonautonomous agent. The agent acts in accordance with her values, but her values are a result of forces external to herself. If, on the other hand, we have no answer of this sort, it seems that the response to the question "Why does the agent have this system of values?" is simply "She just does have it" or "This is just what she is like." But the agent seems equally "stuck with" her set of values on this picture as on the former one; she is thrown into the world, as it were, complete with an identity she did not choose.

In order for an agent to be autonomous, it seems, not only must the agent's behavior be governable by her self, her self must in turn be governable by her self—her deeper self, if you like—and this must in turn be governable by her (still deeper?) self, *ad infinitum*. If there are forces behind the agent, so to speak, making the agent what she is, then her control of her behavior is only intermediate, and therefore superficial. But if there are no forces behind the agent making the agent what she is, then her identity seems to be arbitrary. The ability to act in accordance with a nature or a character—or, for that matter, with an uncharacteristic motive—that one simply finds in oneself as an arbitrary given, seems equally to constitute a merely superficial species of control. But this would seem to exhaust not just the empirical but the logically possible alternatives: Either something is behind the agent, making the agent what she is, or nothing is. The idea of an autonomous agent appears to be the idea of a prime mover unmoved whose self can endlessly account for itself and for the behavior that it intentionally exhibits or allows. But this idea seems incoherent or, at any rate, logically impossible.

The dilemma that was earlier sketched only schematically can now be given a more concrete form: The condition of autonomy seems at once impossible and necessary for responsibility. If there is to be any hope for a positive solution to the problem of responsibility, we must find a way to resist the conclusion that the condition is as it seems. Either this apparently necessary condition must be shown not to be a necessary condition of responsibility after all, or this apparently impossible condition must be shown to be one that, despite appearances, it is possible, and even plausible, to think we regularly satisfy.

Defending the Problem as a Problem: The Metaphysical Stance

I hope that, in light of the dilemma of autonomy, the problems of responsibility and free will, as I earlier characterized them, will seem meaningful and compelling. As I have already declared, my central aims in this book are to provide insight and some degree of relief from these problems. The attempt to achieve these aims will proceed through an examination of the dilemma of autonomy and alternative responses to it. Before I embark on this project, however, there are some general doubts that need to be addressed. For in developing a context that gives life to the problems of responsibility and free will I reveal an assumption that is indicative of a controversial philosophical stance. The assumption is that there is a fact of the matter as to whether we are free and responsible beings, a fact we might discover and about which we might be wrong. From a certain perspective this assumption seems mistaken, and philosophical inquiry into the concepts of responsibility and free will, insofar as it is infected by this assumption, may seem misguided from the start. Those who make this assumption may be said to take a metaphysical stance toward free will and responsibility. Those who oppose it may be said alternatively to take a pragmatic stance toward these concepts.

We may characterize the difference between these two stances by reference to two different kinds of responses we might have when, in the course of our experience, we find ourselves wondering whether we should hold a particular person responsible for a particular act. Sometimes the question of whether we should hold a person responsible for an act seems to demand an answer to a prior question of whether she *is*, in fact, responsible for it. But, in other cases, there seems to be no prior question to be asked—all the facts are in, so to speak, concerning what the person did and what circumstances and psychological events led to her doing it—and all that is left for us, apparently, is the *choice* of whether, in light of these facts, we want to hold her accountable. The metaphysical stance relies on our disposition to respond to cases in the first way, to think that the answer to whether an individual is an appropriate object of certain attitudes and judgments, or a legitimate participant in certain practices, is somehow given to us, even if obscurely, by the nature of the individual and her relation to the action in question. The pragmatic stance, on the other hand, takes the second sort of response to be the more philosophically revealing, for such a response reflects an acute awareness that the attitudes, judgments, and practices whose appropriateness is in question are, after all, *our* attitudes, judgments, and practices—and shouldn't we be able to decide what to count as appropriate and legitimate instances of these in whatever ways we please?

From a pragmatic perspective, then, it appears that whatever facts are relevant to the justification of the activities connected to responsibility are relevant only because we choose to make them relevant, because, in other words, we set up roles that assign these facts a certain weight.

To be sure, the pragmatist will say, we must abide by the rules we establish unless we are prepared, in some general way, to revise them. So that if it is one of our rules that a person is not to be held responsible for actions she is unaware of performing, we must acknowledge that the fact of her ignorance, a fact of which we may be unaware, puts a limit on which judgments and attitudes will turn out to be justifiable. But which facts shall limit the justifiability of our attitudes, judgments, and practices depends on the rules that regulate the formation of these attitudes, judgments, and practices, and which rules regulate the formation of these attitudes, and so on, depends on us.

From the pragmatic perspective, there can be facts of the matter that constrain our attitudes, judgments, and actions insofar as they turn on the question of whether a person in a particular instance is to be accorded the status of a responsible being, but there can be no fact of the matter the discovery of which might undermine the justifiability of these practices as a whole. For if we are committed to a way of life that involves according most adult human beings the status of responsibility—and it seems we are so committed— then we are committed to setting up rules that govern the justifiable attributions of this status in such a way as to make these rules fit—that is, justify—at least the core cases of according this status to normal adults acting in normal situations. If the rules we set up seem to backfire on ourselves, so that by our own rules it appears that none of us are ever responsible, we should not take this as a discovery that we are not, in fact, responsible beings, but rather as a signal that we must revise or clarify our ideas about the conditions of responsibility.

The metaphysical stance toward free will and responsibility assumes there is a fixed fact of the matter about what it is to be a responsible being, though the fact is obscure and philosophical investigation, involving discovery and analysis, is required to bring it to light. Until this investigation is satisfactorily completed, according to this view, it is an open question whether anyone actually is responsible and indeed whether the concept of responsibility is a coherent one at all. According to the pragmatic perspective, however, this view is fundamentally wrong. What is fixed is that we are responsible beings—that is, most of us are, most of the time—and this is fixed not by a fact we happen to know to be true but by a commitment we have to making it true. The philosophical inquiry that is required, on this view, is, in the last analysis, not a theoretical investigation at all, not ultimately a matter of discovery. Rather, it is a practical inquiry involving forward-looking considerations, the ultimate goal of which is to arrive at the best system of rules to govern the practices associated with responsibility in ways most satisfactory to our needs.

There is a truth embodied in the pragmatic perspective which I hope will be, by the end of this book, better understood and given its full weight. But it is wrongly identified if it is understood to imply that we reject the metaphysical question of free will—the question that treats the claim that we have never been and can never be responsible as, at the outset, an epistemological possibility. It is a mistake to treat the question "Under what conditions do people deserve to be held accountable for their actions?" as ultimately and solely dependent on the practical questions of what conditions for desert will contribute to maximally meaningful and rewarding lives and what conditions for desert will most effectively encourage people to be morally good. For although the rules governing the complex of practices that are conceptually held together by their connection to the status of responsibility may not be given to us by "the nature of things" independent of our dispositions and choice, neither are they as flexible as to tolerate the sorts of revision that the adoption of the pragmatic approach would require. However we explain the development of this complex of practices, the development has already taken place. These practices, and the concepts, attitudes, and judgments that form essential parts of them, have established meanings, however obscure, and it is with these meanings that these practices and their components play the deep and pervasive role in our lives that they do.[4]

Even attempts to revise or refine the rules of games like chess and baseball—examples, presumably as pure as can be, of activities whose rules are up to us to determine—are constrained by the requirement that certain elements be preserved, for without them the games in question would no longer be those games. It is an essential feature of the complex of practices associated with responsibility that they be subject to a justification involving reference to the status of responsibility. And it is an essential feature of the concept of responsibility involved that it be one that applies or fails to apply to a person as, in a certain sense, a matter of fact. Thus, the proposal to treat the question of whether we are ever responsible as something other than a matter of fact must ultimately be seen as a proposal not to deal with the problem of responsibility at all. Rather, it is a proposal to look at ourselves and our lives in such a way that the problem of responsibility loses its significance, a proposal that would reassign the significance it formerly had for us to other more tractable problems.

The aptness of this criticism is most clearly evident when it is leveled against philosophers like Moritz Schlick, for whom "the question of responsibility is the question: Who, in a given case, is to be punished?"[5] (or, as he later adds, rewarded). This, as a practical question, amounts to a call to develop the system of rewards and punishments that most effectively encourages people to act well rather than badly. Obviously, basing a decision to punish someone solely on the consideration that by doing so we will better succeed in influencing that person and other members of society to act in morally preferable ways in the future does not provide us with an interpretation of the concept of responsibility. Rather, this decision ignores the question of the agent's responsibility or deems the question to be irrelevant. This approach to the question of punishment and reward would have us understand these practices as species of moral manipulation, no different in kind from the strategies we use to toilet-train children or to tame circus animals. It disregards the difference in meaning we attach to praise and blame when these are expressions of admiration and indignation from the meaning overtly similar activities might have when they are motivated simply by the desire to reinforce or inhibit the kind of behavior in question. Thus, it leaves no room for any importance for the question of whether the agent is responsible. On this view, it does not matter whether the person *deserves* to be punished—if it would be useful to punish him, then we should do so whether or not his punishment is deserved.

Schlick's view, insofar as it is offered as a solution to the problem of responsibility, is naive and simplistic because it fails to recognize that the concept of responsibility is connected to the practices of reward and punishment only by way of and in the company of this concept's connection to subtler, less overt practices that involve attitudes, for example, of admiration and indignation, and judgments of agents' deserts. But one may adopt Schlick's basically pragmatic approach to the concept of responsibility without losing sight of the complexities of the role of this concept in shaping and defining our practices. If one searches for forward-looking reasons for maintaining not only our practices of reward and punishment but also the attitudes and judgments that form a basis for distinguishing between kinds of reward and punishment, one will find them. Just think how impoverished our lives would be if we ceased to take such attitudes and form such judgments—how much thinner would be our sense of self-worth if we ceased to feel pride, shame, and. guilt, and how much shallower our interpersonal relationships if we ceased to admire, respect, feel gratitude, resentment, and indignation toward one another.[6] Since there are forward-looking reasons for preserving the distinctiveness of these attitudes and judgments, it would seem that we can ask how best to preserve them, how best, that is, to set up the rules for these attitudes and judgments so as to encourage us to form them in ways that optimally enhance our sense of the meaning, value and richness of our lives. This more sophisticated form of a pragmatic approach less evidently fails to address the problem of responsibility that is connected to the justification of our practices—but it fails nonetheless.

For the sense that there is a fact of the matter as to whether a person is responsible for his actions, a sense that pragmatic approaches to responsibility either fail to notice or dismiss as confused, is an essential feature not only of the justification of a particular kind of punishment or reward but also of the justification of the attitudes and judgments this punishment or reward might express. We can make the sense in which the question of one's responsibility must be a matter of fact somewhat less abstract if we focus for a moment on a single type of attitude or judgment. Let us focus on resentment.

Clearly, we resent someone only if we think the person has done us some harm or done something that would have been expected to do us some harm. But it is essential to the nature of resentment that it can be deserved or undeserved, appropriate or inappropriate, where the conditions of desert or appropriateness go beyond the establishment of the fact that the person really did perform the action in question and that the action really did, or would have been expected to do, some harm to us. We do not, in general, resent someone who causes us a harm if her doing so was accidental or if she acted in ignorance or if her action was coerced or if she was under hypnosis. Our resentment is conditioned on the belief that in acting as she did she was expressing an attitude toward us of contempt or unconcern—or, at any rate, on the belief that in acting as she did she was failing to express an attitude of respect or consideration that we think she should have had. Moreover, our resenting her rests on the belief that her acting in a way that expresses this attitude toward us (or that reveals the absence of a different attitude toward us) was up to her. That is, we believe she had a kind of control over what she was doing that would have allowed her to take the attitude that we feel was our due, an attitude that, if she had taken it, would have led her to act differently. But there is a fact of the matter as to whether she did have that kind of control of her actions, as to whether the action that offended us was truly up to her in the sense required for her action to reveal an attitude toward us that we regard as insulting.

If we do not care about whether she had the relevant kind of control of her actions, then we do not care whether our resenting her is appropriate. But we cannot be said to be in a state of resenting her at all if we do not believe that our resentment may or may not *be* appropriate. And if we never cared whether our resentments were appropriate, then resentment would lose its distinctness from anger or annoyance or frustration that the world was not behaving as we would like it to behave.

The suggestion that we can decide what shall count as appropriate or inappropriate occasions for resentment would, if taken seriously, ultimately destroy our ability to feel resentment, as distinguished from other negative attitudes. That is, this suggestion would ultimately undermine the possibility of forming the very attitude it tries to legitimate. More generally, the suggestion that we take a pragmatic approach to the set of attitudes and practices associated with the concept of responsibility would, if taken seriously, ultimately undermine the whole complex of attitudes and practices whose preservation this approach is designed intentionally to protect.

The metaphysical stance is appropriate then, because the concepts of free will and responsibility that are already firmly established are intrinsically metaphysical concepts. That is, it is an essential criterion for the correct application of these concepts that they be subject to the demands of justification by the facts. Since we have a substantial interest in living in accordance with the facts, we have a substantial interest in finding out whether, in thinking of and treating ourselves and one another as free and responsible beings, we are living in a way that is justified by the facts or, at any rate, not in contradiction to them. And because the thought, or perhaps the unthought assumption, that we are free and responsible beings plays so important a role in the way we think about ourselves and our relation to the world, the discovery of whether we are (internally) justified in having this thought or making this assumption will presumably lead to a significantly deeper understanding of ourselves.

If the answer to this question is positive, then it is possible that we will gain something more. For a positive answer to the metaphysical questions of free will and responsibility will tell us not only that we are justified but why. That is, it will tell us what features of ourselves are essential to our being free and responsible beings, and this may give us reason to care about these features in a special way and to arrange our lives and our values in such a way as to preserve and promote these features.

But it might turn out that the answer to this question is negative. In other words, we might be forced to conclude that we cannot coherently and justifiably continue to think of ourselves as free and responsible beings. In that case, it will be of great interest to know what deep-seated tendencies in human nature have encouraged and allowed us to be mistaken about so important a matter for so long. But it will also be necessary to come to terms with that conclusion. If we are not free and responsible beings, what then? This last question must be answered from a pragmatic perspective. It is, after all, a practical question. Thus, even from a metaphysical stand-point, the pragmatic perspective must remain available as, so to speak, a last resort. Indeed, there is reason to think that some of the proponents of the pragmatic approach have adopted it precisely because they believe that negative answers to the metaphysical questions of responsibility and free will are unavoidable and be-cause, in light of this, they are impatient with philosophers who continue to seek a more positive conclusion.

This book will not even attempt to refute the view that negative answers to the metaphysical questions of responsibility and free will are unavoidable. To the extent that this book offers answers to these questions, they are answers that will not guarantee that we are, in the full metaphysical sense of these concepts, free and responsible beings. In fact, if the views in this book are correct, there can be no such guarantee. Nonetheless, the book addresses the metaphysical questions in a spirit that takes pessimism about them to be unwarranted, and in the hope that patience, in philosophy as elsewhere, will have its own proverbial rewards.[7]

2

The Real Self View

(In Which a Nonautonomous Conception
of Free Will and Responsibility
Is Examined and Criticized)

In Chapter 1 I presented the related problems of responsibility and
free will as problems the forcefulness and structure of which could
be understood by reference to the dilemma of autonomy. Through
the recognition that autonomy appears at once necessary for responsibility and impossible to realize or achieve, I suggested, the
concepts of responsibility and free will can be seen to be deeply
problematic or obscure. For if autonomy is necessary for responsibility, there is reason to think that responsibility and free will are
impossible. And if autonomy is not necessary for responsibility,
then there is reason to think that we are fundamentally confused
about what responsibility and free will are. In this context, the
question "What kinds of beings must we be if we are ever to be
responsible for the results of our wills?" takes the shape of a
demand to know whether or not we must, in particular, be autonomous beings. And the alternative answers to this question give
structure in turn to the related question of how, if at all, responsibility is possible. For if responsibility requires autonomy, we need to
know how, if at all, *autonomy* is possible. And if responsibility does

not require autonomy, we need to know what features of presumptively nonautonomous beings could give sense and justification to attributions of responsibility to *them*.

Readers who are familiar with discussions of the metaphysical problems of responsibility and free will may be used to thinking about these problems in somewhat different terms. For the "free will debate" that is carried on in philosophical journals tends to focus, not on the connection between free will and autonomy, but rather on the connection between free will and various forms of determinism. To most such readers, the connections between these discussions and the discussion to follow will be obvious. Still, it is worthwhile to make some of these connections explicit, both to better orient the reader and clarify the ways in which these other discussions address and are addressed by this one.

Relating the Problems of Free Will and Responsibility to Determinism

That there is a philosophical problem about free will and determinism can be explained as a result of the following two facts: On the one hand, the claim that we are free and responsible beings seems incompatible with the claim that determinism is true. On the other hand, determinism, or some form of it that seems incompatible with free will and responsibility, seems likely, or at any rate not unlikely, to *be* true. This poses a dilemma that is formally similar to the dilemma of autonomy. If free will and responsibility are incompatible with determinism, then there is reason to think that we may not be free and responsible beings. But if free will and responsibility are compatible with determinism, then we need to know more about what free will and responsibility are that will explain why the appearance of incompatibility is so persistent.

Once this dilemma is posed, however, we can see that we need to know more about what free will and responsibility are in any case. For we cannot discover whether free will and responsibility are compatible with determinism without a better understanding of these concepts. That is, before we can answer the question of whether free will is compatible with determinism, we need a conceptual analysis, or elaboration, of the concepts of free will and responsibility that will make the essence of these concepts, so to speak, more apparent in terms that will allow the question more readily to be grasped. Indeed, insofar as the debate about free will and determinism is a coherent and unified one, some such analyses or elaborations must be already implicitly at work. That is, the incompatibilists, as they are called, must share a common conception of free will and responsibility, in virtue of which they take the application of these concepts to be incompatible with determinism, and the compatibilists, insofar as they form a unified group, must share some general beliefs about why the incompatibilists' conceptions of free will and responsibility are mistaken.

The suggestion that the problems of free will and responsibility can be structured by reference to the dilemma of autonomy implicitly offers an interpretation of what contrasting conceptual analyses underlie the debate about free will and determinism. According to this interpretation, incompatibilism (or the predominant form of it) is grounded in the belief that autonomy is required for responsibility and that autonomy is incompatible with determinism. Compatibilism, by contrast, issues from a view according to which autonomy is not required for responsibility and according to which what is required is clearly compatible with determinism's being true. In other words, the suggestion is that most incompatibilists are incompatibilists because they have autonomous conceptions of free will and responsibility, and most compatibilists are compatibilists because they have nonautonomous conceptions of these notions of a kind that raise no *prima facie* problems with respect to their compatibility with determinism.

The plausibility of this suggestion can best be evaluated only after the autonomous and nonautonomous conceptions of free will and responsibility are more fully laid out. I hope and expect that compatibilists will be able to identify their positions in the nonautonomous conceptions of free will and responsibility I will explore in this chapter and that incompatibilists will be able to identify their positions with the autonomous conceptions of these notions I will explore in the next. But it should be acknowledged at the outset that proponents of autonomous and nonautonomous conceptions of free will and responsibility are not logically committed respectively to advocating incompatibilism and compatibilism. It is possible to believe that autonomy, though necessary for free will and responsibility, is compatible with determinism. In fact, Kant and Sartre, two of the most compelling defenders of autonomous conceptions, both seem to have views of this sort. And it is possible to believe that although autonomy is not required for responsibility, what is required is also incompatible with determinism. Though at this point this view may seem to have little to recommend it, reasons for taking it seriously will emerge as the discussion proceeds.

Avoiding Autonomy: Developing the Idea of an Agent's Real Self

We may now return to the problems of responsibility and free will as they are structured by reference to the dilemma of autonomy. Since the condition of autonomy seems at once necessary for responsibility and impossible to realize or achieve, a defense of the possibility of responsibility must take one of two possible paths: Either it must provide a nonautonomous conception of responsibility or it must provide a coherent and realizable conception of autonomy. Recalling the way in which we were led initially to accept the condition of autonomy gives us reason to attempt to construct a defense along the former path first. For we were led to accept the condition of autonomy in an effort to explain the intuitive appropriateness of exempting agents in certain exceptional situations from responsibility. Accepting this condition, however, seems to lead to the counterintuitive (and highly undesirable) conclusion that all agents are always exempt from responsibility, or perhaps that the very concept of responsibility makes no sense. Thus the condition of autonomy, which was attractive because it seemed to offer an explanation of some of our intuitions, turns out (apparently) to explain too much. It seems natural to doubt our purported explanation before we doubt the deeply entrenched belief that an acceptance of this explanation seems rationally to require.

Reexamining our purported explanation, we can see why it explains too much. It is because the features of the agents and their situations on which we focused in the attempt to explain why in these exceptional cases the agents were not responsible for their actions turned out, on examination, to be features that were common to exceptional and nonexceptional cases alike. But while victims of hypnosis, coercion, and mental illness are, in some respects, just like our normal selves, it is also clear that in some respects they are quite different. If we can find an alternative explanation for our intuitions regarding these exceptional cases that focuses on features that distinguish these examples from ones more typical of adult human life, then we may be able to formulate a more lenient condition of responsibility that, in accordance with our intuitions, excludes the agents in the problematic examples without threatening our claim to be, by and large, and in most situations, responsible beings ourselves.

To this very purpose, David Hume suggested an alternative explanation which other philosophers of mind have subsequently elaborated and refined. Hume acknowledged, as we did, that cases of the sort illustrated by the three cases described earlier are problematic because the agents in these cases had to perform the actions they did—because, in other words, these actions were necessitated by forces in some sense external to the agents themselves. But, Hume points out, there are two senses of "necessity," which our previous response to these problematic cases failed to distinguish. On the one hand, there is a sense of "necessity" that seems "to imply something of force, and violence, and constraint," to which "the liberty of spontaneity" may be said to be opposed; on the other hand, there is a sense of "necessity" that is inextricably connected to the idea of causation, to which "the liberty of indifference," but not the liberty of spontaneity, is opposed. According to Hume, it is the former kind of necessity that makes the problematic cases problematic, and this should suggest that the kind of liberty opposed to it— the liberty of spontaneity—is a condition of responsibility. Failing to notice the difference between this sense of necessity and the sense connected to the idea of causation, however, we misidentified the problematic elements in the cases above and thus mistakenly formulated the condition of autonomy that requires the responsible agent to have not the liberty of spontaneity but the liberty of indifference.[1]

Of course, the ideas of "force, and violence, and constraint" are themselves in need of clarification if Hume's claim that only these sorts of causes are incompatible with responsibility is to seem plausible. If this claim is to provide a basis for explaining the case of hypnosis, "force" must not be restricted to *physical* force; and if it is to provide a basis for explaining the case of kleptomania, "constraint" must not be restricted to observable, *external* constraint. Nonetheless, it seems true that all these cases contain features that deprive the agents in them of a kind of liberty that we normally have—features, in other words, that interfere with or inhibit the agents' normal abilities to control their behavior in accordance with the values and choices of their deepest selves. Perhaps the best way to clarify the notion of "constraint" that is relevant to a defense of Hume's view is by offering a characterization of these normal abilities and a model of action that involves the free exercise of them. Then constraint may be defined as anything that prevents the agent from conforming to this positive model.

In a sense, I have already suggested a very simplistic positive model of this sort: Under normal conditions of freedom, an agent is able to govern her behavior on the basis of her will, which in turn can be governed by the set of the agent's desires.[2] But recalling the cases of hypnosis and kleptomania yet again, we can see that this model is too simplistic to separate the normally free actions from the ones that are intuitively unfree. For these cases remind us that there are occasions when an agent may be constrained by her own desires, and situations in which an agent may feel forced to act from a will that, in one sense but not in another, is not her own. An agent, in other words, may be alienated from her own desires or from her own will. In some cases—for example, the kleptomaniac case—the agent might say that she would not have the desire in question if she could choose. In others—the hypnosis case might serve as an example—the answer to whether the agent would have the desire if she could choose may be indeterminate. The agent's alienation from her desire arises rather from the recognition that her choice is irrelevant—that, in other words, her having the desire in question is independent of her choosing to have it. In still other cases, the agent may not feel alienated from her desires at all, but may feel alienated from her will, because she would not have chosen to act on her desires in the way she did. A dieter, for example, might identify with her sweet tooth and yet prefer to refrain from indulging it. When she accepts the offer of dessert anyway, she does so "despite herself," feeling, perhaps, compelled by (what is admittedly) her own desire for sweets.

An agent does not have absolute authority over the question of what desires and actions are to be identified with or deeply attributed to her. An agent who claims to be moved by a desire that is not her own may be in bad faith; an agent who regards herself as a victim of internal compulsion may be merely a victim of self-deception. Conversely, an agent may regard herself as a fully responsible agent acting from desires that are wholly her own, and yet be compelled or constrained by forces of whose power or existence she is unaware. (The influence of alcohol or drugs provides ready examples of this.) Although these facts point to the considerable difficulties involved in establishing the claim that an agent is acting under undue constraint, they are irrelevant to our present task of analyzing the meaning of such a claim.

Whether or not the agent who claims to be acting from an inner compulsion is right, we may ask what it would mean for her to be right, for by doing so we may refine our positive model of unconstrained human action, which, prior to the intrusion of philosophical thinking, seemed intuitively free enough for the agent to be justifiably held responsible for it. We have already agreed that this agent is at liberty to perform whatever action she wills to perform—what she thinks she lacks, and what she may truly lack, is the liberty to will whatever action she wants to will.[3] She is alienated from her will, because her will is not, in an important sense, the result of her choice.

We might try to characterize the positive model from which the actions of this agent diverge as one according to which the agent acts according to her will, and the agent wills according to her choice. But there are reasons for finding this characterization unsatisfactory. For if an agent can be alienated from her will, one might think, she can also be alienated from her choice. Indeed, one might think that if an agent performs an action intentionally—that is, as a result of her willing it—there must be some sense in which she chooses to perform it. So if she is alienated from her will, then she *must* be alienated, in that sense, from her choice. Of course, one might say that the unfree agent does not choose to make *that* choice, thus locating the distinction between the unfree and the free at one level further down, as it were. But this begins to make our positive model look implausible. For we do not naturally think of our ordinary actions as resulting from a *series* of choices: we do not ordinarily choose to choose to will to act. And even if there are some exceptional situations in which it makes sense to characterize an agent in this way, this characterization will not distinguish the free agents from the unfree. For an agent who is alienated from her first-order choice may be alienated from her higher-order choices as well.

It would be better, then, to characterize our positive model, from the beginning, in terms not of the quantity of choices underlying the action the agent ultimately performs, but rather in terms of the quality of the choices, however many there are. The crucial feature distinguishing unalienated from alienated action is that the will (or the choice, or the multitude of choices) of the unalienated agent arises from the agent's unalienated self—from her real self, if you will, the self with which the agent is to be properly identified. Our positive model of action, from which the apparently unfree actions discussed above can be seen to diverge, must be a model according to which the agent's actions are governed by her will and her will is governed by her unalienated, real self. Obviously, our positive model must include some characterization of an agent's real self, a characterization that avoids the temptation to distinguish what is from what is not a part of that self by reference to whether the aspect of the agent in question is one the agent has chosen to have.

Gary Watson[4] has suggested that we can provide the characterization we are after if we recognize the difference between what he calls the agent's values, on the one hand, and the agent's desires, on the other. Or rather, since the agent's values are themselves desires of a certain kind, the distinction of importance is that between the agent's values and the rest of the agent's desires. According to Watson, an agent values something (whether an object, a state of affairs, a disposition, or whatever) if she thinks it good, or if she thinks there is some reason to want it. By contrast, an agent may want something that she does not think it is good to have or want; indeed, she may be motivated to attain some object while at the same time believing that it would be wholly bad or wrong to attain it. Watson points out that such unvalued desires may be impulsive and transient, as, for example, the desire to drown one's baby in the bathwater, or the desire to smash the face of one's squash competitor with one's racket. Others may be long-standing, dispositional desires, such as the desire to smoke cigarettes, or the desire to sleep with one's best friend's spouse. Desires that are not values are desires we may be indifferent or even uncomfortable about having—the prospect of satisfying such desires may not be preferable to the prospect of eliminating these desires in other ways. Our values mean more to us than that—it will be important that they be satisfied rather than otherwise eliminated, and, if they cannot be satisfied, we may even prefer the prospect of living with the discomfort of unsatisfied desires to the prospect of ceasing to have these desires at all. (Consider, for example, our attitudes toward the desires for justice and love.)

If the distinction between values and desires is to serve as a basis for understanding what a person's real self is, Watson's own characterization of this distinction must be slightly modified. For the identification of a person's values with what that person thinks good or supported by reason unconditionally puts a person's reason, or her faculties of judgment, broadly construed, at the core of the person's real self. Indeed, Watson acknowledges his debt to Plato's division of the soul into Reason and Appetite and suggests that values correspond roughly to those desires which have the support of or their origin in the agent's Reason. Admittedly, many people, and particularly many philosophers, are likely to identify their deepest selves with their faculties of reason. But there are some who trust their hearts more than their minds, and it is not incoherent for a person to care deeply about something and yet be uncertain as to whether she thinks the thing she cares about is good. It is possible for a person to embrace a commitment to a principle, person, or group, and yet lack the ability and even the inclination to justify that commitment. We can, however, construe the notion of values somewhat more broadly, as comprising those things which a person cares about, or alternatively, as including all and only those things which *matter* to a person in some positive way, without losing the distinction between what a person values and what she merely wants, or desires, or likes.

In light of this, it seems plausible to distinguish those desires which are part of the agent's real self from those which are not according to whether the desires in question are also values for the agent. But our primary concern is to understand not which desires but which actions may be attributed to the agent's real self, and, although there is promise to the suggestion that the right class of actions is made up of those actions which arise out of the agent's values, this suggestion must be elaborated and made more precise if it is adequately to capture the class we have in mind.

An agent who has values will almost certainly value some things more highly than others, and, when values compete, the relative weights she assigns them will inform her judgment about what, all things considered, is the thing for her to do. Just as there can be a disparity between what an agent values and what she desires (and is therefore to some extent motivated to do), there can be a disparity between how highly an agent values something and how strongly she is motivated to pursue it. In accordance with the distinction between values and desires, Watson distinguishes between valuational and motivational systems. An agent's judgments of the form that, all things considered, X is the thing for her to do, arise out of the agent's valuational system. An agent's will, however, depends on what the agent is most strongly motivated to do, and this may or may not accord with the agent's valuational judgment. Thus, the dieter mentioned earlier might not only desire but truly value the appreciation of a fine chocolate mousse, in addition to valuing the attainment of a lower body weight. Then it would be true in a sense that whether the agent takes the mousse or not, her action could be said to arise out of her values. But if the judgment that issues from the agent's valuational system would have her refrain from eating dessert, it is understandable that the agent who takes the dessert anyway might think herself constrained by her own values.

This suggests that we can more accurately characterize the class of actions that are attributable to an agent's real self as the class of actions that arise, not simply out of the agent's values, but out of her valuational system. But if we are to identify the class of actions that are attributable to the agent's real self with the class of actions for which we ordinarily consider ourselves responsible, this characterization still needs to be amended. For the suggestion that all the actions that are truly mine arise out of my valuational system seems to endow my actions generally with a more profound significance than they typically have. When I pour myself a second cup of coffee, or put on a sweater, or walk to the subway, I am not ordinarily expressing deeply held values or judging at all whether, all things considered, my action is a worthwhile or good one to perform. Although, in the absence of a special context, it would be strange for someone actively to claim responsibility for actions of this sort, it would be stranger still to deny responsibility for them. Moreover, an action that is not in accord with my valuational system may seem at least somewhat significant precisely because that action is attributable to me. I may, for instance, hold myself responsible for the weakness of my will or for my lack of self-discipline.

These facts are easily explained if we recall that the positive model we have been trying to characterize is a model of acting with the full range of *liberties* that we ordinarily think ourselves to have. For what seems crucial to our sense of responsibility for the kinds of actions just described is that, whether or not our actions *are* governed by our valuational systems, there seems to be nothing that *prevents* our actions from being so governed. In other words we are, or think we are, at liberty to exercise valuational judgment, and to make such judgment effective in governing our behavior; the full resources of our valuational systems are, as it were, *available* to us as agents, use them as we may.

Thus, we may say that an agent's behavior is attributable to the agent's real self—and therefore that the agent behaves as she does in the absence of undue constraint—if she is at liberty (or able) both to govern her behavior on the basis of her will and to govern her will on the basis of her valuational system. On the other hand, an agent may be said to be unduly constrained if something inhibits, interferes with, or otherwise prevents the effective exercise of these abilities.

Using this definition of constraint, we can explain the cases that earlier troubled us along the lines that Hume suggested. For the victims of hypnosis, coercion, and kleptomania all do seem constrained. These agents do seem unable to govern their actions on the basis of their respective valuational systems. The kleptomaniac's will and the will of the person who is under hypnosis are governed by desires that are presumably not among the agents' values at all. And even if the desires that move the victim of coercion are also values of hers, it is not the importance of the values but the strength of the desires that determines the content of

her will. Of course, for these agents to be truly constrained, it must
be the case not only that their actions *are* not determined by their
valuational systems but that they *cannot* be. But it is plausible to
think this is true of the agents in the cases at hand. For it is plausible
to think that the agents in these cases are either in situations that
inhibit their ability to make valuational judgments at all or are in
the grip of desires so strong as to compel them to act as they do,
whether they value these actions or not.[5]

Because the agents in these cases are unduly constrained, their
actions are not attributable to their real selves. And the fact that
their actions are not attributable to their selves seems to justify our
intuition that they are not responsible for their actions. Moreover,
the notion of a real self may be used to throw further light on our
intuition that lower animals and young children are not responsible
for their actions. For lower animals and young children do not seem
to have real selves—they do not, or not yet, have valuational
systems, as distinguished from a mere set of desires, and so there is
no possibility that their actions can be in accordance with them.

Thus the suggestion that an agent is responsible only for those
actions which are attributable to her real self, understanding an
action to be attributable to one's real self only if in performing it
one is at liberty to govern one's actions on the basis of one's
valuational system, seems at once to unify and to comprehend all
our intuitive responses to cases we have considered thus far. Every
agent we have considered who does not seem to be responsible for
her actions either lacks a real self entirely or lacks the freedom to
express it. By contrast, most fully developed human beings seem to
have real selves which, in ordinary circumstances, they are at liberty
to express and, more generally, to use in governing their behavior.
Thus, unlike the requirement of autonomy, the requirement that an
agent's behavior be attributable to the agent's real self is a condition
of responsibility that can explain and justify our tendency to think
that some agents are not responsible for their behavior without
throwing doubt on the possibility that any agents are.

The view that the attributability of an agent's behavior to her real
self constitutes a necessary and sufficient condition of responsibility
offers us an alternative to the view that responsibility requires
autonomy. For this view does not require an agent to be endlessly
accountable to herself—that is, it does not require that her self be

governable by her self *ad infinitum*. It is required that an agent *have* a real self, and that she be able to govern her behavior in accordance with it. But it does not matter where her real self comes from, whether it comes from somewhere else or from nowhere at all. Let us call this the Real Self View.

If Hume is right, then our earlier inclination to accept the condition of autonomy was just a mistake, based on a confusion between the idea of causation and the idea of constraint. In light of our analysis of constraint, we may relate this confusion to a different one—namely, the confusion between the idea of a person's real self and the idea, so to speak, of her undifferentiated self. In any case, it may appear that the reasoning that led us to accept the condition of autonomy was persuasive only because we failed to recognize the psychological complexity of the human agent. Failing to recognize relevant differences among the ways in which an agent might be caused to will to act, or to recognize relevant differences among the types of control that an agent might have, we misidentified the source of our thought that the agents in the three problematic cases discussed were not responsible for their actions. Attending to these complexities, we should be able to see that the problems lay not in *whether* but in *how* the actions in these cases were caused. That is, the problems had to do not with the ultimacy but with the type of the agents' control of their behavior.

Problems with the Real Self View

Despite the attractiveness of this view, the doubts that earlier beset us might reasonably remain. For even if the three problematic cases that originally led us to formulate the condition of autonomy can be explained without appeal to this troubling condition after all, other problematic cases cannot be so comfortably disposed of. Moreover, once the idea of autonomy was introduced, it seemed to make an intuitive kind of sense that it should be a requirement of responsibility, and the intuitive fittingness of this requirement does not vanish when we attend, as Hume suggested, to the distinction between causation and constraint, or when we attend to the distinction between a person's real self and the rest of her psychology. If the tendency to think that autonomy is necessary for responsibility is based on a confusion, the confusion must be deeper than the ones that have been suggested, and it is hard to see how the alternative view that an agent is responsible if and only if her behavior is attributable to her real self can provide a basis for unmasking this confusion, if it is one.

It will help us to understand these objections more fully, if we call attention to the central place the Real Self View gives to the point of view of the agent in determining whether the agent is responsible for her actions. For if the condition that the agent's actions be attributable to the agent's real self is to serve not just as a necessary but also as a sufficient condition of responsibility, then it follows that any agent who has a real self is responsible at least for any action that is actually governed by her valuational system. Thus any agent who has a real self is responsible for any wholly unalienated actions, for any actions that the agent would, on reflection and in light of relevant information, unqualifiedly regard as actions that are truly hers.

It does not follow that an agent will be an absolute authority as to whether she is responsible for her actions. For, if weakness of the will is possible, then an agent may be responsible for an action from which she feels (and, depending on how one defines one's terms, from which she may truly be) alienated. For she may be at liberty to act in accordance with her valuational system and yet act in a way that does not so accord. Conversely, an agent may think she is responsible for an action for which she is not, for an agent may be unaware of factors that alienate her from her actions. While under hypnosis, for example, an agent may not be able to recognize a discrepancy between her values and the motives she is hypnotized to have. And she may never recognize this, if she never learns that she was hypnotized or if she never comes out of her hypnotized state.

Still, an agent will generally be able to tell whether she is alienated from her actions or not, and, with the exception of certain cases of weakness of the will, an agent's own disposition to regard an action as an expression of her real self will, on this view, conform to an objective assessment of the agent's responsibility for it. In light of this, we can see why this view can account for the three problematic cases above. These are all cases of agents whose actions are in potential conflict with the judgments of their real, unalienated selves. Moreover, we can see why this view can account for the majority of problematic cases that are apt to come to mind. For we are rarely disposed to question the responsibility of an agent who does not question it herself.

Nonetheless, we sometimes do question the responsibility of a fully developed agent even when she acts in a way that is clearly attributable to her real self. For we sometimes have reason to question an agent's responsibility *for* her real self. That is, we may think it is not the agent's fault that she is the person she is—in other words, we may think it is not her fault that she has, not just the desires, but also the values she does. There may be forms of insanity that give rise to these thoughts. For although many mental disorders may, like kleptomania, leave a large part of a person's independently identifiable real self intact, and others may undermine a person's capacity to have any unified real self at all, there is no reason to think it impossible for mental illness to take the form of infecting someone's values in such a way that the self with which the victim completely and reflectively identifies is a self that other persons reasonably regard as being drastically mentally ill. (The Son of Sam murderer who made headlines some years ago might be an example of this sort.) Similarly, whether or not hypnosis is necessarily limited to transient effects on a mere portion of an agent's psyche, we can easily envision other forms of psychological conditioning (consider, for example, Orwell's *1984*) that could make more permanent and pervasive changes in the most central features of a person's self. Finally, and perhaps most disturbingly, there are persons whose values we are apt to explain as resulting from deprived or otherwise traumatic childhoods—persons who have fully developed intelligences and a complete, complex range of psychological structures, levels, and capacities for judgment, but who nonetheless do not seem responsible for what they are or what they do.

The claim that the sorts of people just described are not at all responsible for some of the actions that arise out of their real, unalienated selves is admittedly controversial. Some people think that such persons are somewhat responsible for the actions in question, but less responsible than they would be if they had not been afflicted with the deprivations or diseases or otherwise traumatic experiences of the kind I have mentioned. It should be noted that this weaker claim is enough to cast doubt on the claim that an agent is responsible for all and only those actions which are attributable to the agent's real self. For the agents in question seem fully to have real selves, with which their actions are wholly in accord. That is, they have fully developed psyches, with valuational systems, as distinct from motivational systems, that are as well-defined in their cases as in others, and with the same abilities to make valuational judgments, to use reason and argument, and so on. In this respect, they are different from children. And the actions in question are actions that, by hypothesis, they wholly want and choose to perform. If they had conflicting thoughts before performing these actions, these conflicts were resolved *in favor of* performing them, and if they later have regrets, these regrets are like the regrets we have when, as wholly unconstrained, unalienated agents, we do something that we later wish we had not done. Since these actions, then, are wholly attributable to these agents' fully developed real selves, on the view we are now considering one would expect these agents to be wholly responsible. If these agents are less than wholly responsible, this view must be leaving something out.

There are some, however, who do think such people are wholly responsible for their actions. They believe that no answer to the question of how someone's character or real self was formed could possibly lessen that person's responsibility for the actions that are "truly his." To the suggestion that such considerations might be mitigating factors, at least one philosopher has replied:

> He did not make his character; no, but he made his acts. Nobody blames him for making such a character, but only for making such acts. And to blame him for that is simply to say that he is a bad act-maker.[6]

I must confess that I feel an unbridgeable gulf between this point of view and my own. This breakdown of shared intuitions seems to indicate a difference in outlook so basic as to leave little hope of finding a more basic common ground to which both parties can appeal. Of course, it is easy to say that philosophers like Hobart (the author of the passage quoted above) have forced their intuitions into conformity with an otherwise attractive philosophical picture—that, in other words, they are in the grip of a philosophical picture that subverts their ability to evaluate objectively the sorts of cases that should serve as tests for that view. But such claims can be made from either side of the dispute.

Because the case of the victim of the deprived childhood, and other cases that are relevantly similar in form, are typically controversial, it would be wrong to place too much weight on one's intuitions about these cases. The character of the controversy, however, is revealing in a way that is independent of its settlement, and attention to it may help us express more general reasons for being dissatisfied with the Real Self View. For the fact that some people are reluctant to regard the agents in these cases as responsible beings is enough to motivate the question of why these agents are responsible beings, if in fact they are. The reply that these agents are acting in accordance with their real selves only begs the question at this point, restating the condition that, if offered as a sufficient condition of responsibility, is itself in need of support.

Nonetheless, defenders of this position often admit that they have nothing else to say, and express puzzlement over the fact that others still feel something is missing. This seems to indicate that defenders of this position think they have reached rock bottom in our potential for understanding the nature of responsibility. For them, the attributability of an agent's behavior to an agent's real self is not just a necessary and sufficient condition of responsibility, it is more like a definition, which captures the meaning of "responsibility."

If we read the passage quoted above with a particular emphasis, the view seems attributable to Hobart:

> He did not make his character; no, but he made his acts. Nobody blames him for making such a character, but only for making such acts. And to blame him for that *is* simply to say that he is a bad act-maker.

We can understand this remark as an indication of a more general view: To be a responsible agent is simply to be, as it were, a fully formed act-maker. A bad act-maker deserves to be blamed; a good one deserves to be praised. And a maker of acts that are neutral in value may simply be acknowledged as such.

If this is the view to which proponents of the Real Self View are, or ought to be, committed—if, in other words, this is the view that

provides the most coherent and plausible defense of that position—
then we have reason to reject it. For it is just not true that to blame
someone for an action is simply to say that he is a bad act-maker.
At least it is not true of the particular kind of blame that is
associated with the philosophical question of responsibility.

Earthquakes, defective tires, and broken machines are, at least
sometimes, bad act-makers, as are dogs and children and adults
with various physical and mental handicaps. But we do not blame
them, at least not in the way in which we sometimes blame normal
adult human beings. More generally, inanimate objects, natural
phenomena, lower animals, and normal adults in a wide range of
contexts exhibit all sorts of behavior that can be seen to have all
sorts of positive, negative, or neutral value. We can recognize that
these individuals behave in these ways, and recognize that their
behaviors have the values they do, and yet find it completely inappropriate to blame or praise or otherwise attribute responsibility to
these individuals for the behaviors in question.

The ability to express this point clearly is complicated by the fact
that we sometimes use the word "responsibility" simply to identify
what we may call the primary causal agent(s) of an event or state of
affairs. For example, "the bent axle is responsible for the noise the
car is making," "the muddy track is responsible for the horse's poor
performance," "the beautiful weather is responsible for the picnic's
success." We may even "blame" the car's noise "on" the axle, or say
that we have the good weather "to thank." But this use of "responsibility" and related words and phrases seems different in kind from
the uses that are understood when we are considering questions of
moral responsibility; and it is easy to construct examples in which
an individual is responsible for an event in the former sense but not
responsible for it in the latter.

We may refer to the former sense of "responsibility" as superficial
responsibility, and, in connection with this, we may speak of superficial praise and blame. When we say that an individual is responsible for an event in the superficial sense, we identify the individual as
playing a causal role that, relative to the interests and expectations
provided by the context, is of special importance to the explanation
of that event. And when we praise or blame an individual in the
superficial sense, we acknowledge that the individual has good or
bad qualities, or has performed good or bad acts. But when we hold

an individual morally responsible for some event, we are doing more than identifying her particularly crucial role in the causal series that brings about the event in question. We are regarding her as a fit subject for credit or discredit on the basis of the role she plays. When, in this context, we consider an individual worthy of blame or of praise, we are not merely judging the moral quality of the event with which the individual is so intimately associated; we are judging the moral quality of the individual herself in some more focused, noninstrumental, and seemingly more serious way. We may refer to the latter sense of responsibility as deep responsibility, and we may speak in connection with this of deep praise and blame.

While moral responsibility is probably the least controversial and best-examined species of deep responsibility, there may be other species of deep responsibility, or other contexts in which we attribute deep responsibility to agents as well. At least some of the judgments we make when we evaluate an individual's intellectual, physical, and artistic accomplishments seem to involve attributions of credit or discredit that are not reducible to an acknowledgment of these individuals' causal roles. (Recall, for example, the contrast between the child's fingerpainting and the more mature artist's watercolor.) And qualities like courage, patience, arrogance, closed-mindedness, which are not moral qualities in the narrow sense of that term that connects morality to benevolence or impartiality, may yet serve as the basis for deep compliments and criticism that are of, as opposed to merely about, the person in question.

There may be no clear or sharp line separating the deep instances of praise and blame or other attributions of responsibility from the superficial ones, and there may be no clear or sharp line separating the instances when deep, as opposed to merely superficial, praise, blame, and the like would be appropriate. Nonetheless, the difference in character between these two kinds of responsibility cannot be denied. For it is intelligible to wonder whether a person is deeply responsible for an action even after we have removed all doubt that she really did perform that action. We can coherently acknowledge that a person really did play a relevantly crucial role in bringing a very good or very bad event about, and yet be uncertain about whether the person deserves to be praised or blamed for it. In other words, we can understand that a person is superficially responsible for the effects of her behavior and yet wonder whether and why that person should be considered deeply responsible for them. So that with respect to deep praise and blame, it cannot be the case that to blame (praise) someone *is* simply to say that she is a bad (good) act-maker.

A defender of the view under consideration might try to invoke a distinction between act-makers and Act-makers. Full-blown Act-makers, or Agents, are not just identifiable individuals who some-how or other produce effects—they are individuals with selves, indeed, with real selves, and the effects they produce can properly be called their Acts only if these effects are related to their real selves in specifiable ways. But the suggestion that we can under-stand the difference between superficial and deep responsibility simply by attending to the distinctively interesting and complex relation that agents with real selves may have to some of their acts will not do. For the difference between superficial and deep respon-sibility is not simply a difference between a general relation and a more specific and particularly interesting and complex species of that relation. It is rather a more dramatic difference in kind—a difference, as the labels suggest, in depth.

The set of instances of deep praise and blame is not simply a subset of instances of praise and blame more generally that take a particular class of agents as their objects under conditions in which these agents perform their acts in a particular way. If it were, then the difference between deep and superficial praise or blame would be merely a difference in the precision with which we identify the cases of recognizably desirable or undesirable events, and expres-sions of deep praise or blame would differ from expressions of superficial praise or blame only in offering different amounts of information about what objects and what processes involving those objects played particularly crucial roles in bringing about those events. It would be the same kind of difference, then, as the differ-ence between our blaming an accident on a car, as opposed to its driver or the weather, and our blaming it more precisely on the left front tire, and, more precisely still, on a defective tire, rather than an old one or one that has been improperly attached to the wheel. But the characters of deep and superficial attributions of praise, blame, and responsibility differ in a more fundamental way: Deep attributions seem to be more serious than superficial ones; they seem to have a different and special significance.

When we subject a person to deep praise and blame, we regard that person in a different light from that in which we regard other objects whose qualities and effects we can evaluatively assess. When we hold a person deeply responsible for things, we understand her to be accountable for them in a different way from that in which other objects can be accountable. It is only in the context of this distinctive kind of accountability that the question of whether an individual *deserves* praise or blame, or of whether she should be given credit or discredit *for* her recognizably good or bad features or actions, makes sense. It may be that the class of deeply responsible agents coincides exactly with the class of agents who have real selves, and that the class of actions and qualities for which these agents are deeply responsible coincides exactly with the class of actions and qualities that proceed from the agents' real selves in the sense already described. But, even if this were so, we would need an explanation of why these classes coincide. Why should the distinctive kind of complexity that is constituted by the possession of a real self make a person subject to a different kind of accountability from that to which other creatures and objects are subject? Why should the fact that a person's real self is superficially responsible for an event imply that, in addition, the person is deeply responsible for that event?

Attention to the psychological complexities that are distinctive to persons does not yield an answer to these questions. Such attention may help us explain why, if any individuals are deeply responsible, they will be individuals with real selves and with the ability to govern their actions and characters on the basis of them. But it will not explain why we think that any individuals are deeply responsible at all, and it will not provide us with a means of discovering whether this thought is coherent or justifiable.

The view that deep responsibility is equivalent to attributability to an agent's real self is incomplete without an explanation of why this equivalence holds. It cannot offer a solution to the problems of free will and responsibility without such an explanation—without, as it were, an explanation of why real selves should also be deep selves.

The controversial examples of victims of comprehensive insanity, psychological conditioning, and dramatically deprived childhoods suggest that, in fact, real selves may not always be deep selves. In other words, they suggest that some individuals with fully developed real selves may not deserve praise and blame for what they do and what they are.[7] If they do deserve praise and blame—or if they do not but there are others who do—we need to know why they deserve these things. But to do this, we must go beyond an examination of the internal complexities of a particular class of agents and consider the relation these agents, by contrast to other agents, have to the world in which they act.

Enlarging the scope of our vision in this way, searching for a difference in the relations between an agent and her world that could account for the difference in depth, seems to draw us irresistibly to a reconsideration of the condition of autonomy. For the inclination to regard the victim of a deprived childhood as an individual who is not responsible for her behavior arises from the thought that, though she acts from a fully developed real self, she is not responsible *for* that real self. That is, she is not in control of who she ultimately is, and thus when she acts in accordance with her real self, her actions are the mere unfolding of the inevitable role she is fated to play in the blind, ceaseless flow of the world's events. Clearly, the kind of control of who the agent ultimately is that we feel to be lacking cannot be supplied by the addition of another loop to the internal structure of the agent. But if the difference between agents who have and agents who lack this kind of control is not a difference in the complexity of the kind of control an agent has over her character and her acts, one might think that it must be a difference in the ultimacy of the agent's control. And this is precisely what distinguishes autonomous agents from all others.

Autonomous agents, unlike other agents, are neither inevitable products of the inevitable interactions among things in the world that exist prior to themselves, nor brute existents whose natures are arbitrarily and unalterably given to them. Autonomous agents choose what role they will play in the world, so to speak; they act not only *in* the world but *on* the world, from a position that allows them a point of view that is, at least in part, independent of the world. Autonomous agents, then, have a kind of control over their behavior that is different in kind from the control that other agents have, and it is plausible to regard this difference in kind as, in some sense, a difference in depth.

A satisfactory theory of (deep) responsibility must not only be able to identify which agents are responsible, and for what—it must be able to explain why they are responsible, and, ultimately, why the idea of responsibility makes any sense at all. In the absence of such an explanation, the view that responsibility is equivalent to attributability to an agent's real self cannot even be regarded as a candidate for a satisfactory theory of responsibility. The idea of autonomy seems to offer a possible basis for such an explanation, which defenders of the view under consideration might try to make use of to fill the gap that must be filled. But in that case, the view under consideration would be not an alternative to the view that connects responsibility to autonomy but rather an elaboration of a particular form of that view.

3

The Autonomy View

(In Which an Autonomous Conception of Free Will and Responsibility Is Examined and Criticized)

Chapter 2 explored an attempt to develop a nonautonomous conception of responsibility in the hope that it would lead us away from the dilemma of autonomy. The attempt focused on the differences between the internal structure of an agent who possesses and is at liberty to exercise the powers of a fully developed person and the structure of agents who lack some of these powers or the liberty to exercise them. In particular, it noted that unlike other agents who are merely able to have and to act in accordance with desires, unconstrained persons are able to have and to act in accordance with values. Had this difference provided a sufficient basis for making sense of and justifying attributions of responsibility, the Real Self View would have enabled us to leave the problematic idea of autonomy behind.

But, although the development of the Real Self View brought with it significant insights, it fell short of realizing the hopes that motivated it. For although it explained apparent differences in responsible status between fully developed unconstrained persons and others, it failed to explain apparent differences in status among fully developed unconstrained persons themselves. And although

46

the fact that persons and only persons can act in accordance with values, as opposed to desires, seems relevant to attributions of responsibility, this attempt failed to explain *why* it is relevant, and so failed, at a fundamental level, to explain why responsibility makes any sense at all.

The conception of responsibility developed in Chapter 2 thus leaves important gaps to be filled, and they are gaps for the filling of which the condition of autonomy naturally resuggests itself. With respect to the dilemma of autonomy, then, we seem to be back where we started: If autonomy is not necessary for responsibility, it remains to be shown why it is not. If autonomy is necessary for responsibility, it remains to be shown how autonomy, and so responsibility, can be understood to be coherent and realizable. The fact that the attempt of Chapter 2 to develop a conception of responsibility that would avoid the condition of autonomy fell short in no way implies that all attempts of this sort must be unsuccessful. But the persistence of the apparent connection between responsibility and autonomy may suggest that our hopes are better placed along the other path.

We were initially discouraged from taking this path by a consideration of how we tend to understand rational human action. Specifically, it seems natural to think of rational human action as action that is in accordance with what the agent most strongly desires—or, perhaps, in light of what was said in Chapter 2, in accordance with what the agent most highly values. And when we go further and ask why the agent most strongly desires, or most highly values, what she does, we are apt to look for our answer in some combination of the agent's heredity and environment.

But if we find such an answer, then the agent seems to be a mere intermediate link in a chain extending from her heredity and environment to her ultimate behavior. Her actions seem to be a mere unfolding of an inevitable role she is fated to play in the flow of the world's events. But if, on the other hand, we do not find an answer, then the fact that the agent has the values she does seems to be inexplicable. If the agent's role in the world is not fated and inevitable, it seems arbitrary and accidental. If we are to conceive of ourselves as autonomous agents, both these alternatives must be rejected. The difficulty of conceiving of a third alternative is what makes autonomy seem impossible.

It may be noted however, that this reasoning takes place from a point of view external to the agent. When we view our choices and actions from the inside, so to speak, attending to our subjective experience as agents, this reasoning seems less compelling. For at least some of the time, our experience of choice does not fit either of the alternative accounts of it that, from the standpoint of the observer, may appear to be exhaustive.[1] Some of the decisions we make seem neither inevitable nor arbitrary. They do not seem inevitable because it seems that even when all the reasons, desires, and other external factors that influence me are taken into account, two or more alternative courses of action or paths of behavior remain open to me. That is, it seems that I can do (or could have done) one thing *or* another. Yet they do not seem arbitrary, for the ultimate selection of which alternative I take seems to issue, positively and actively, from me: I *make* the decision or choice of what to do—the choice does not merely befall me.

On examination, it may turn out that these experiences are not accurately characterized as experiences of autonomy. That is, it may turn out that the conception of ourselves that having these experiences seems to presuppose is not, after all, a conception of ourselves as autonomous beings. And if there is a conception of ourselves as autonomous beings that we sometimes have, or that we might have, it may turn out that this conception is a false one, that the experience of autonomy is an illusion. But these possibilities can be evaluated only after some phenomenological investigation has been done.

By focusing on our subjective experiences as agents, we can at least try to develop a conception of autonomy—we can try, that is, to develop a conception of what an autonomous agent would be like, and leave the problem of reconciling such a conception with an observer's perspective until later. In fact, I shall argue that we need never reach this problem. This problem will cease to be of interest. For as we develop a conception of what an autonomous agent would be like, we will come to see it as something we don't particularly want to be like, and, more to the point, as something we don't need to be like in order to make sense of and justify our sense of ourselves as responsible beings. But this, too, must await the results of some phenomenological investigation.

The Apparent (but Only Apparent) Autonomy of Valuing Selves

To carry this out, we may begin where we left off at the end of Chapter 2, with the suggestion that the idea of autonomy be used to supplement and enrich the account of the fully developed and unconstrained person that was elaborated in that chapter. The suggestion is a natural one, I think, because the distinction between values and desires, of which the account in Chapter 2 made so much, calls to mind a conception of ourselves according to which, at least at first glance, the idea of autonomy appears to ring true.

The difference between values and other desires, remember, is a difference not in content but in source. The same object of motivation may be merely desired by one person and valued by another, and what is valued at one time may be merely desired (by the same person) at another. Values differ from other desires in being motivations that we not only have but care about having. They are motivations that matter to us, that we think it somehow good or important that we have. Using the vocabulary of Chapter 2, values are motivations that arise out of or are supported by an agent's real self.

The aspect of our practical lives that the distinction between values and desires is designed to capture is most explicitly revealed when there is a divergence between what we desire, or most strongly desire, and what we value, or most highly value. We are apt to think first of conflicts between values and desires that have a strong phenomenological aspect to them, of situations in which we are conscious of desires that, by an effort of will, we must overcome or resist. I battle with the temptation to open the box of Godiva chocolates that I mean to give away as a housegift. I force myself out of bed in order to get to my lecture on time. By contrast with values, desires that are not valued are often quite recognizably *passions*. They are states that are imposed on us, or that, at any rate, we find ourselves at least momentarily "stuck with."

What values we have, on the other hand, seems to be a matter of choice. For although it is not a prerequisite of an agent's having a value that that value have been self-consciously embraced, it must be true, barring problematic cases involving self-deception, that if the question arose, the agent *would* embrace it. And it is natural that when we survey our experiences for concrete examples of our valuing selves, we focus on those occasions—which are after all not so rare—when we do reflect on what we care about and embrace some objects or principles as values. We may be struck by the thought that we are letting our lives be guided by principles and goals we have unthinkingly adopted. And we sometimes find reasons to accept new principles and goals that call for a reexamination of our habits. Thus, for instance, a person might consider, and reject, her parents' value in chastity before marriage. Another might recognize the degree to which her life is dominated by a concern for professional status, and decide to alter her behavior in ways that put this interest into what she regards as a more sensible perspective. One thinks about and decides whether to become a vegetarian, and whether to make efforts to rid one's prose of sexist language.

The picture that develops out of attention to these experiences is one according to which our valuing selves may seem to *rise above* our more brutish, desiring selves. As valuers, it seems, we are able to take stock and survey our desires and dispositions, rejecting some perhaps as utterly worthless, and ranking others in ways that may take account of but need not ultimately reflect their relative motivational strengths. Moreover, our deliberations about value may lead us to adopt new interests and principles that, prior to deliberation, we had no motivation whatsoever to pursue or obey. Our desires may even seem to have the status of data, which our valuing selves are able to assess. They suggest possible objects of value to us, but we are never required or compelled to adopt them.

On this picture, our merely desiring selves may well seem to us to fit the picture of our whole selves that the observer's perspective suggested. For on this picture our valuing selves are, in a sense, themselves observers (and judges) of our merely desiring selves. Our merely desiring selves, then, may well seem to be either the inevitable product of the influences of our heredity and environment or arbitrary collections of random dispositions and other properties. If we were nothing more than our desiring selves, it might be granted, we would not be free and responsible beings. But because we are able to form and act on values, we are able to transcend this aspect of our existence.

It is tempting, in light of the contrast between our valuing and our merely desiring selves, to identify our valuing selves with autonomous selves. For in some sense in which we cannot help having the desires we have, we can help what values we have. In some sense in which we are stuck with our desires, it seems, we have a choice about our values. And when we focus on those occasions in which we actively think about and decide what values to embrace, it seems that prior to our thought we *can* take one path *or* another—we can affirm the values of our parents, for example, or reject them—and yet what path we do take is hardly accidental, for our choice arises out of and is explained by our reflections and deliberations.

It is doubtful, however, that the sense in which we seem to have a choice about our values is properly characterized as an experience of autonomous choice. For the idea that we choose what to care about and what to do in a way that is independent of or, at any rate, not necessarily determined by the force of our unvalued passions may yet be interpreted in a way that suggests that our choices are determined by something else.

Indeed, the imagery evoked by the claim that our ability to form values allows us to *transcend* our merely desiring selves suggests that we have this ability in virtue of having something else— namely, a faculty or method for making judgments and decisions that is somehow higher than the faculties, methods, and other processes by which our mere desires and other dispositions are formed. In light of the fact that our ability to form values is in addition associated at least hypothetically with the activities of reflection and deliberation, it would not be unnatural to refer to this "higher" faculty as Reason—practical reason, that is, under- stood in a way that ascribes to it some substantive, more than instrumental, content. The sense in which we cannot help having the desires we have but can help what values we have may then be interpreted as a reference to the fact that our values, unlike our mere desires, can be controlled or chosen in accordance with Rea- son. Our valuing selves may then be identified with our rational selves.

If we do identify our valuing selves with our rational selves, however, it remains an open question whether our valuing selves are autonomous. For the ability to act in accordance with Reason may seem to free us from one threat to autonomy only at the cost of making us susceptible to another. We have already seen that an agent who acts in accordance with her desires—an agent, in other

words, who does what she most wants to do because she most wants
to do it—may not be an autonomous agent. For if she cannot help
having the desires she has and she cannot help acting on her
strongest desires, then she is not in ultimate control of her actions.
If Reason is similarly a property or faculty that an agent cannot
help having (or lacking), and if it generates motives that an agent
cannot help acting upon, then an agent who acts in accordance with
Reason is likewise not in ultimate control of her actions.

Though the principles and goals that govern the rational agent
may differ in character from those which govern a non-rational
agent—perhaps they will be higher or better principles and goals—
they may govern her no less strictly. Insofar as we identify ourselves
more closely with our Reason than with our nonreasoned desires,
we may regard rational action as more wholly ours than nonreasoned action would be. But if it is not up to us to *be* rational agents,
and if, being rational agents, it is not up to us to have and to act on
the reasons we have, then action in accordance with Reason is no
more autonomous than action in accordance with any other psychological process would be.

At least some of our experiences of choosing what values to have
and what values to act on—experiences that encourage a conception of ourselves as agents who are free from manipulation by our
passions—are nonetheless compatible with the thought that we are,
if not manipulated, at any rate, inseverably bound or unavoidably
governed by our Reason, or, less pretentiously, by our reasons. We
do, after all, sometimes speak of being moved, or even compelled,
by Reason. And we sometimes speak of reasons as *making* us
choose one action rather than another. When I resist my temptation
to eat chocolates, it is true not only that I cannot help admitting the
existence of a passion for chocolates but also that I cannot help
noticing the tightness of my jeans. The possibility that, in light of
the latter recognition, I could not help choosing to resist the chocolates is not eliminated by appeal to my introspection alone. Nor,
when I question the values of my parents or colleagues, does my
introspection tell me whether I could have helped questioning them,
or whether, having questioned them, I could have helped (let us
suppose) rejecting them. Perhaps my observation of others who live
by different values or my friend's arguments in support of different
values *made* me question my parents' values. And when I did

question them, perhaps I could not help discovering that the reasons against their values were stronger than the reasons for them. Finally, once I have discovered that Reason favors one conclusion over the other, perhaps I have no choice but to adopt the conclusion that my Reason supports. It is certainly hard to imagine discovering that my parents' values are insupportable, and *then* choosing to make them my values despite their irrationality.

The idea that prior to one's deliberations about values one *can* choose one set of values or another is compatible with the idea that one cannot help engaging in deliberation and that, posterior to this, one *must* choose one set rather than another. Our experience of choosing in accordance with Reason is silent on the question of whether, insofar as Reason supports one alternative over all others, we can help choosing that alternative. Since, if we cannot help choosing the most rational alternative, we are not autonomous agents, our experience of ourselves as rational agents cannot properly be characterized as an experience of autonomy.

Autonomy as the Ability to Make Radical Choices

A truly autonomous agent would be no more bound by Reason than by Desire. Thus, a truly autonomous agent must have a freedom more radical than that which the ability to act in accordance with Reason automatically affords. The ability to act in accordance with Reason might be said to free one from having to act in accordance with mere Desire, but, to be autonomous, one must also be free from having to act in accordance with (mere?) Reason. Obviously, the ability to act in accordance with Reason is not capable of freeing one from that. Nor will it do to postulate some faculty still "higher" than Reason, in virtue of which the agent can transcend the status of being merely Rational. For if there were some higher faculty, then autonomy would also require that the agent be free from having to act in accordance with that faculty. One would have to go on postulating higher and higher faculties *ad infinitum*.

We may as well understand "Reason" to refer to the highest faculty or set of faculties there are, the faculty or set of faculties, that is, that are most likely to lead us to form true beliefs and good values. If we understand Reason in this way, the autonomous agent must be one who is able to act in accordance with Reason *or not*. That is, she must be able to regard the rational course of action, insofar as there is one, as just one alternative among others. We have seen, moreover, that this ability to choose among the rational, irrational, and nonrational alternatives alike is not an ability to choose on some higher-than-rational basis. Rather, it is an ability to choose on no basis whatsoever, an ability, if you will, to choose whether to use any basis for (subsequent) choice at all.

Admittedly, this ability to make radical choices is somewhat opaque. Since a radical choice must be made on no basis and involves the exercise of no faculty, there can be no explanation of why or how the agent chooses to make the radical choices she does. Still, we occasionally do find ourselves with choices that no amount of deliberation can settle, choices in which the reasons for two or more alternatives are equally strong or incommensurable, or in which our wills simply fail to be engaged by the consideration that a certain alternative is more rational. From the inside, it would seem that we make these choices on no basis. We seem simply to make them. And in more usual situations, when we do make rational rather than radical choices, the thought that we nonetheless have the ability to choose differently is easy enough to conceive.

When, for example, I am offered an apple and, being hungry and liking apples, I take one, I am aware of no compulsion that forces me to take it. No constriction of the throat makes it evidently impossible for me to say "No, thank you." Similarly, when I jump into the ocean to save a drowning child, the child's cries do not seem irresistibly to impel my feet from the shore. Thus, it is easy to suppose that even when we do choose on the basis of Reason—when, at least, we choose the most rational alternative—we nonetheless possess the *ability* to choose otherwise. It is easy to suppose, in other words, that though we do act rationally we do not have to so act. To suppose this is to suppose that we have the ability to act in accordance with Reason or not. In other words, it is to suppose that we are truly autonomous agents. Though the ease of supposing this does not make it true, this is not to the present point. For the moment, I want to consider not whether we *are* autonomous agents, but only what we would be like if we were, and whether, in light of this, we have reason to want to be autonomous agents.

We have now developed a conception of what autonomous agents must be like: They must be agents who not only *do* make choices on no basis when there is no basis on which to make them, but who also *can* make choices on no basis even when some basis is available. In other words, they must be agents for whom no basis for choice is necessitating. If the balance of reasons supports one alternative over all the others, it is still open to them to choose whether to act in accordance with the balance of reasons or not. We must now consider whether we have any reason to want to be autonomous agents.

The (Non)Desirability of Autonomy

Certainly, we have reason to want to be able to make choices on no basis when there is no basis on which such choices can sensibly be made. In situations in which the reasons for several alternatives are equally strong or incommensurable, it would be better to be able to choose on no basis than to remain paralyzed like Buridan's ass. But here what we want is the ability to choose, not the ability to choose *on no basis*. For the absence of a basis for choice is not, in these cases, a reflection of our powers as agents. It is rather a feature of our situations, and a typically unhappy feature at that.

To want autonomy, then, is not only to want the ability to make choices even when there is no basis for choice but to want the ability to make choices on no basis even when a basis exists. But the latter ability would seem to be an ability no one could ever have reason to want to exercise. Why would one want the ability to pass up the apple when to do so would merely be unpleasant or arbitrary? Why would one want the ability to stay planted on the sand when to do so would be cowardly or callous?

One might think that the ability to pass up the apple might come in handy another time, when, for example, there were not enough apples to go around; the ability to refrain from saving the child might be just what would be needed on a different occasion, when others would save the child and one would more usefully see to the safety of the children remaining on shore. Of course, it is reasonable to want the ability to respond differently on different occasions, but to want this is to want not autonomy but the ability to respond as the occasion demands. To want this is in fact just to affirm one's desire for the ability to act in accordance with Reason, since what act is in accordance with Reason will depend on what situation one is in. To want autonomy is to want the ability to make a more fundamental choice, the choice of whether to act in accordance with Reason or not. To want autonomy, in other words, is to want not only the ability to act rationally but also the ability to act *ir*rationally—but the latter is a very strange ability to want, if it is an ability at all.

To see this as an ability one might want to exercise, one must view the possibility of acting irrationally as potentially desirable. In other words, one must think that irrational action may be as attractive as rational action. If one thinks that acting with Reason may be no better than acting against Reason, then one can see the ability to choose whether to act with or against it as an increase of options that intelligent and perceptive agents might intelligibly want to exercise.

One might, of course, characterize oneself as wanting the ability to act against Reason, if one identifies Reason with certain concrete forms of thought and argument the relative value of which one questions. "Reason" is sometimes contrasted to emotion, for example, and associated with exclusive attention to precise logical argument and a preference for thinking in quantitative terms. A person who always consults and acts according to Reason in this sense might be found unattractively cold, straitlaced, lacking in spontaneity.

"Reason" as it is being used in this book, however, is an explicitly and essentially normative term. It refers to the highest faculty, or set of faculties, there are—that is, to whatever faculties are properly thought to be most likely to lead to true beliefs and good values. In light of that, any attempt to offer reasons for wanting to act against Reason will only show that the sense of Reason under attack is not the sense intended.

Keeping in mind the essentially normative character of "Reason," the claim that one might intelligibly want to act in defiance of it must be understood as a way of denying that there really is such a thing as Reason in that sense at all. It is a way of expressing a position of radical skepticism, or nihilism, about the objectivity of values. For the point being made is that one has no reason, so to speak, to obey the dictates of Reason, that this allegedly higher faculty is not really higher, that the suggestion that there are higher faculties is a myth.

Radical skepticism about values, then, does offer a context in which the ability to act independently of Reason can be seen as an ability that one might intelligibly want to exercise. But this position has problems of its own, and, at any rate, it is incompatible with an interest in or even comprehension of the concept of responsibility with which this book is chiefly concerned. These issues will be discussed in the last section of this chapter, and again in Chapter 6. Before addressing them, let us consider a different point of view that might seem to give one reason to value autonomy.

One must be a skeptic about values if one is to regard the ability to make choices independently of Reason (as Reason is here being used) as an ability that one might intelligibly want to *exercise*. But one might think that a nonskeptic has reasons to value this ability as well. For one might value *having* the ability to act against Reason even if one conceives no possible desire to exercise it. If we focus on the example of the swimmer, for instance, who is urged by Reason to save the drowning child, we can imagine two apparently different kinds of interest in the ability to act against Reason by remaining on shore. The value skeptic might want this ability because she might, after all, want to remain on shore. And why not? For although there is Reason to save the child, the skeptic sees no reason to take Reason seriously. There are no objective normative considerations to tilt the balance of her choice either way. But a nonskeptic might acknowledge the reasons for saving the child in a way that would affirm her commitment to acting on them and yet might still value the ability to choose differently. For though she might have every intention of saving the child, she might not like the idea of *having* to save it.

Why should one want an ability that one never wants to exercise? Why should one care about being locked in a room—or better, in a world—out of which one cannot *conceivably* want to go? Why should one mind if, to put it in extreme terms, one is *inescapably* sane?

Perhaps the nonskeptic will explain that, though she values the life of the child, she also values her own freedom of choice. Unlike the skeptic, she believes that there is a right and rational decision, and she hopes that she will make it—but she also hopes that the decision will be truly up to her. Whether the ability to act against Reason contributes to her freedom of choice, however, whether it bears positively on her decisions' being truly up to her, is precisely what is at issue.

The position we are considering assumes that one's freedom of choice would be compromised if one's choice necessarily followed one's Reason. It assumes that insofar as one's Reason is unconditionally decisive in determining one's choice, to that extent the choice is not truly and ultimately one's own. These assumptions reveal an implicit conception of Reason as alien to oneself, as a determining force with which one might in principle be in competition. But, holding fast to the broad and essentially normative use of the word Reason, it is not clear that such a view is intelligible.

The thought that some concretely specifiable set of considerations absolutely determine one's choice may naturally suggest a restriction on one's freedom, a limitation on one's ability to see and consider acting upon any considerations that lie outside of that set. But in the case of being determined by Reason, no considerations, at least no rational or reasonable considerations, lie outside of the set. For to be determined by Reason is to be determined by whatever reasons there are. To be worried about being determined by Reason seems comparable to being worried about being blind to what doesn't exist. But this is at best a stretched sense of blindness, and one that would be far from obviously regrettable.

Perhaps the best way to evaluate what bearing the ability to act against Reason has for one's freedom and control is to see what the possession of this ability might amount to in concrete circumstances. Let us return to the lifesaving example, or rather, to two lifesaving examples alike in every respect except for the presence or absence of this ability in their protagonists. Both cases involve equally strong swimmers, who know equally little about the child struggling in the water. In both cases, there are relatively few other adults around, none closer to the water, and so on. In each case, the woman (or man) in question hears the child's cries and more or less immediately moves into action. Neither engages in conscious deliberation, but both have been sufficiently educated and trained to have cultivated dispositions to recognize and respond to situations like this without need of deliberation. The difference between the two cases consists solely in the fact that the first agent, unlike the second, did not *have* to jump in. Despite the existence of clear and decisive reasons to save the child, the first agent, unlike the second, could have remained on shore. Perhaps the first agent could have thought "I won't do it," whereas, for the second, given the circumstances, such an idea was unthinkable. But one could equally suppose that the second agent could have had the thought—she simply could not have taken the thought seriously.

Should one wonder why the first agent differs in this respect from the second, a number of possible answers suggest themselves. Perhaps the first agent had learned the lesson of the importance of human life less well—perhaps she was less convinced than the second agent that the value of saving a stranger's life outweighs the value of keeping her hair dry or finishing her conversation. This difference in conviction might in turn be traced back to a difference in upbringing or in natural character. Alternatively, the conviction of both agents might be equally strong—both might unfailingly recognize that right Reason favors saving the child. The hold of right Reason on the first agent, however, might simply be weaker than it is on the second. The first agent's will might just be less fully engaged by her Reason than the second's, and again this might be due to a difference in training or a difference in character, or even quite inexplicably due to nothing noticeable at all. What is essential is that, for whatever reason, the first agent, unlike the second, can reject her Reason, and thus the first agent, unlike the second, is an autonomous agent.

The question we must ask is whether, in light of the difference between the first agent and the second, the second agent is any less responsible for her action than the first. Since, by hypothesis, both agents do act in accordance with right Reason and swim out to save the child, the question is whether the first agent deserves a kind of credit or praise that the second does not. I do not see how she can. For, as it happens, each agent acts in accordance with Reason, or, at any rate, in accordance with dispositions earlier cultivated and accepted as a result of her Reason. Each agent acts, in fact, in exactly the way we want agents to act and for exactly the motives we want agents to have. At first glance it seems that each agent deserves as much credit as an agent in this situation can possibly deserve. The difference between the first agent and the second is that the first could have acted *less* well, for *less* admirable motives. Her virtue, in some sense, is less sure than the other. But how can this make her *more* praiseworthy?

One suggestion might be that since the virtue of the autonomous agent is less sure, her choice to act virtuously must involve an inner struggle, an overcoming of temptation that the second, nonautonomous agent is spared. Leaving aside the question of how much praise an agent deserves for successfully resisting the temptation to let a child drown in order to save her coiffure, however, the suggestion is unjustified. For the difference between an autonomous and a nonautonomous agent cannot lie in a difference in inner struggle. By hypothesis, both agents are alike, not only in their possession of reasons to save the child, but also in their possession of reasons, however trivial, not to save it. If we imagine the first agent to have battled temptation, we may imagine the second to have done so as well—their difference lies in the fact that the second was *determined* to conquer it, while the first was not. If, on the other hand, we imagine the second agent to have acted from an unconflicted desire to save the child, so we may imagine the first. That I can make one choice or another does not mean that the choosing must be difficult.

Alternatively, one might suggest that even if the internal experience and the external behavior of the two agents in question are identical in apparent virtue, the fact that the first agent and not the second is autonomous reveals a difference in real virtue. For one might take the fact that the second agent cannot help choosing the virtuous action as an indication that the second agent acts only mechanically, that she acts out of obsessive or, at any rate, blind habit, and thus exercises no (good) judgment of her own. This suggestion fails, too, however, because mechanical action is properly opposed not to autonomous but to rational action, and our examples concern agents who differ in autonomy but not in rationality.

Of course, the case we have been considering is a case of emergency in which near-reflex action is needed. There is no time to exercise subtle powers of discrimination or refined faculties of judgment. But this feature is common to the situation of the autonomous and the nonautonomous agent alike. Both must act equally mechanically if they are to act well, and so both must deserve equal amounts of credit. If, moreover, we move to a nonemergency example in which time for reflection and deliberation is available, we can see that again the nonautonomous agent need act no more mechanically than the autonomous agent; the actions of the former may be as finely cued to subtle perceptions and sophisticated patterns of reasoning as those of the latter. For, again, the difference between the autonomous and nonautonomous agents lies not in their capacities *to* use Reason, but in their capacities to reject Reason.

Since the nonautonomous agent, like the autonomous agent, *can* act in accordance with Reason, the fact that she cannot help choosing the virtuous action indicates only that her Reason supports the virtuous action and that she cannot help acting in accordance with her Reason. We cannot coherently interpret action that results from this process as mechanical, obsessive, or blind. We cannot coherently contrast such action with action resulting from the agent's own judgment—on the contrary, such action seems to be the very paradigm of action *based* on judgment. Thus, it seems, there is no basis for withholding credit from the nonautonomous agent that one is willing to reward to the autonomous agent who performs the same action for the same reasons. Since an agent deserves credit for something only if that agent is responsible for it, this implies that responsibility does not depend on autonomy.

I have exhausted all the reasons I can think of for believing that responsibility requires not just the ability to act in accordance with Reason but also the ability to act against it, for believing, that is, that responsibility requires not just rationality but (radical) autonomy. Still, I know that some people with strong incompatibilist intuitions will remain unconvinced. In the absence of further reasons for this, two explanations seem possible. One is that despite intentions to the contrary, some people continue to lapse into a reified use of "Reason," understanding by it something potentially alien to their deepest selves or even something wholly fraudulent. This would reveal a latent moral and evaluative skepticism in the background of their thinking about freedom. I will turn to this in the next section. A second possibility is that those who continue to insist that radical autonomy is necessary for responsibility do so not because they disagree with my view that the ability to act in accordance with Reason is sufficient for responsibility but because they think this ability itself requires at least a kind of radical autonomy. That is, they believe that the possession of true rationality requires a kind of agency incompatible with ordinary sorts of physical and psychological determination. Though the discussion of ability and possibility in Chapter 5 may have some bearing on this suggestion, the idea remains an interesting one, which I have not fully or directly explored. In what follows, however, I shall return to the use of "autonomy" as referring to something beyond what is required to act in accordance with Reason. Specifically, autonomy requires the ability to act against Reason as well.

A Last Voice in Favor of Autonomy: The Skeptic's Perspective

The line of reasoning presented above would put the project of grounding attributions of responsibility on the possession of autonomy once and for all to rest, were it not for the availability of one final objection. I claimed that, since a nonautonomous agent can act in accordance with her Reason, her actions cannot be regarded as obsessive or blind or as coming to pass independently of any exercise of judgment that can be called her own. In light of this, I argued, the fact that the autonomous agent can in addition reject her Reason adds nothing of value to her condition in virtue of which her actions can be seen to take on a greater significance or her choice to perform them to deserve a deeper kind of praise. But, one might object, one *can* see the nonautonomous agent who acts in accordance with Reason and cannot act otherwise as obsessive and blind *if* one sees Reason itself as either an incoherent myth or an intrinsically worthless psychological trait. If one sees Reason in this light, one can see the nonautonomous agent who is irrevocably attached to her Reason as a hopeless dupe, unconsciously trapped by the prejudices of her time. In that case, only the autonomous agent, who has a healthy detachment from her Reason (and from any other faculties that purport to inform her that some values and choices are better than others) makes choices in a context free of bias, maintaining control over her faculties rather than letting her faculties control her.

If one sees Reason in this light, then one can take the actions of the autonomous agent to be more deeply hers than those of the nonautonomous agent in question, whose actions, after all, are the inevitable consequence of the "rational" values her heredity and environment have programmed her to have. The autonomous agent is not bound by these values, or by any set of values. Her choices emanate from her bare, free self, uncoerced by internal or external forces that would threaten to dictate her decisions. If one sees Reason in this light, one can see the autonomous agent as capable of deserving a kind of credit that the nonautonomous agent cannot deserve. For the autonomous agent can exhibit a kind of strength or wisdom in resisting the claims of false Reason and in retaining the power of choice for her pure, nonrational (or Ur-rational) self.

There is, then, a possible position according to which the possession of autonomy would serve as a kind of ground for a kind of responsibility, a position according to which autonomy would be seen as something importantly desirable. But this position involves a rejection of the power of Reason, or any other faculty or set of faculties, to provide us with a basis for forming better values rather than worse ones. It involves the denial of any possible grounds for thinking that there *are* any better values or worse ones. It involves a commitment to a nihilistic stance on values.

We might note, to begin with, that such a commitment is morally repellent. For it insists that one set of values is objectively as good as any other, regardless of whether it includes, for example, any concern for human liberty or equality or happiness. Such a commitment amounts to a denial that there is any reason for preferring justice to injustice, or kindness to cruelty. More to the point, the kind of responsibility that, according to this position, autonomy would give us would not be the same kind of responsibility that it was our original project to try to secure. Thus, even if the moral objections to accepting this position could be suspended, it would offer no solution to the problem of responsibility that is the focus of this book.

The problem of responsibility with which we have been concerned is the problem of explaining how persons can coherently be understood to have a special status in virtue of which the good and bad things they do can resound to their respective credit or discredit while lower animals and objects cannot be so deeply evaluated for the good and bad traits they display. How can persons deserve a special and deeper kind of praise for being generous or brave than

pictures deserve for being beautiful or cats for having grace? How
can persons deserve a distinctive and more serious kind of blame
for being deceitful or petty than pigs deserve for being sloppy or
books for being frayed?

The position that bases responsibility on autonomy, far from
giving a positive answer to these questions, denies that persons do
deserve praise or blame for the qualities mentioned above. For the
position in question involves a commitment to skepticism about
values, and this implies that there is nothing particularly good
about being generous or brave and nothing particularly bad about
being deceitful or petty. If the autonomous agent deserves praise,
on this view, it is not for saving a child or telling the truth. It is not,
more generally, for arriving at the best decision or for making the
right choice—for on this view, there *is* no best decision or right
choice. (There might be a more rational choice, but the rational is
no better than the irrational.) If the autonomous agent deserves
praise for anything, in fact, it cannot depend on *which* choice she
makes at all, but rather on how she makes it. Since the only thing
that sets the autonomous agent apart from other agents is her
autonomy itself, the only thing for which the autonomous agent
might deserve a special kind of praise is the property of *being* self-
consciously autonomous. In other words, if the autonomous agent
is susceptible to a special kind of praise, it must be praise for the
self-conscious exercise of her autonomy, for the making of radical
choices in full light of the absence of intrinsically worthwhile reasons for these choices.

If one takes in the full implications of the implicit commitment to
value skepticism, however, one realizes that the sense in which an
autonomous agent might deserve praise even for the self-conscious
exercise of autonomy must be different from the sense that we
ordinarily attach to the idea of a person's deserving praise. For
ordinarily a person is understood to deserve praise only if she
exhibits a good trait or performs a good action. It is her possession
of the trait or performance of the action that *justifies* the praise. But
a value skeptic must deny knowledge of the existence of any "good"
traits or actions, *including* the trait of recognizing the absence of
any (other) good traits and the action of choosing in light of this
recognition. From the point of view of a value skeptic, in other
words, no value or set of values can ultimately be justified as

superior to any other, and this includes the value of being, and acting like, a value skeptic.

In fact, most skeptics about value do seem to admire the trait of actively living one's value skepticism, of living, that is, in full consciousness and acceptance of the belief that one's actions and values are wholly one's own, ultimately unsupportable by anything but one's own unjustifiable choice. In Heidegger's vocabulary, this is the trait of "authenticity"; in Sartre's, it is "good faith." From their perspective, it amounts to a kind of honesty with oneself. There seems to me to be nothing inconsistent in this pattern so long as one avoids the suggestion that one's preference for this trait over its opposite is any better justified than more conventional preferences for kindness, justice, and the like. But if one denies the justification for one's preference in authenticity, one necessarily attenuates the sense in which the authentic agent *deserves* blame, Sartre, for example, writes

> Suppose someone says to me, "What if I want to be dishonest?" I'll answer, "There's no reason for you not to be, but I'm saying that's what you are, and that the strictly coherent attitude is that of honesty."[2]

Though the end of Sartre's answer may sound like blame, its beginning raises a question about whether Sartre can coherently regard the blame as deserved. For although the claim that the strictly coherent attitude is that of honesty seems to urge us to *be* honest, Sartre admits that, from his point of view, there's no reason *not* to be *dis*honest.

The only position according to which autonomous agents can coherently be regarded as more responsible than nonautonomous agents, then, is not a position according to which this greater or deeper responsibility can be understood to justify susceptibility to greater or deeper kinds of praise and blame or to greater or deeper attributions of credit and discredit. Though autonomous agents can be said to be more responsible than nonautonomous agents in the sense that only they can be regarded as ultimate sources of their own choices, independent of both the desires and the reasons that their heredities and environments have instilled in them, this sense of responsibility is, so to speak, *merely* causal. No opportunities or powers that can coherently be justified as valuable can be conditioned on this kind of responsibility.

Insofar as we do ordinarily value responsibility for the powers it affords—the power, for example, to make something of ourselves, to raise ourselves up through our own efforts, to achieve an ideal formulated by our own active intelligence (and so to be, at least in our minds, deserving of a deep kind of praise)—it is not the above kind of responsibility, based on autonomy, that we value. For these powers do not require the radical freedom to act against or ignore one's Reason, but only the more moderate freedom to exercise Reason and act in accordance with it. But we have seen that the latter freedom and the responsibility that attends it are compatible with a lack of autonomy.

If, recognizing this, one continues to value the additional freedom that autonomy affords, the freedom, that is, to act against one's own Reason, then either one implicitly embraces the position of moral skepticism, or one must in consistency admit that one's value is unjustifiable and that no one else has any reason to share it.

Since the problem of responsibility with which this book began was the problem of understanding what features could possibly afford us a status that we do think people generally have reason to value—a status that goes hand in hand with the power to achieve a deeper kind of praise and blame than that to which other creatures are susceptible—a continuing concern with the problem of responsibility leads us finally away from autonomy. For we have seen that autonomy, far from being necessary to our concern, is actually irrelevant to it. Even if we do, or can, have the freedom to act against our Reason that only autonomous agents have, this freedom cannot be the basis for the kind of responsibility that we aim to understand. A more moderate kind of freedom, the freedom to exercise and act in accordance with Reason, is emerging as the possible feature of agents that is more to the point. It is to this kind of freedom that we turn in the next chapter.

4

The Reason View

(In Which Another Conception of Free Will and Responsibility Is Proposed)

In the early part of Chapter 3 we saw that the ability to act autonomously could be confused with the ability to act in accordance with Reason. Once these abilities had been distinguished, moreover, we saw that the latter seemed more relevant to our status as responsible agents than the former. For within the class of agents who share the ability to act in accordance with Reason, the difference between autonomous and nonautonomous agents consists in the former's having the ability to act in *dis*cordance with Reason, an ability that at best seems irrelevant to our status as responsible agents and at worst bespeaks a position directly incompatible with that status.[1] If one has the ability to act in accordance with Reason, in other words, it seems that one may be responsible even without being autonomous. We might also point out that if one lacks the ability to act in accordance with Reason, one cannot be responsible even if one is autonomous. For dogs and psychopaths might conceivably be autonomous in the sense that they might be ultimate sources of their own actions, able to act on no basis. But because they lack the ability to act on a basis—in particular, the basis of

67

Reason—they are not responsible in the sense that would allow them to be deserving of deep praise and blame.

The purpose of this chapter is to argue that the ability that is crucial to responsibility is in fact the ability to act in accordance with Reason, as opposed to both the ability to act in accordance with one's Real Self (discussed in Chapter 2) and the ability to act autonomously (discussed in Chapter 3). A better understanding of this position will emerge from a comparison between this view and the two views discussed previously. I will argue that this view preserves the insights of each of these earlier views while avoiding their respective failures. Finally, once the overall thrust and spirit of this view have been conveyed, its implications for specific cases and its ability to explain and accord with our intuitions regarding these cases will be examined.

The Reason View Compared with the Autonomy View

Let us begin by comparing the present view, that a responsible agent is one who has the ability to act in accordance with Reason, with the view discussed in Chapter 3, that a responsible agent is an autonomous agent. The latter view we might redescribe as the view that a responsible agent must always be able to do one thing *or* another. The agent must not be necessitated by causes, Reason, or anything else, to take action along a particular path. To put it still another way, this view amounts to the position that no matter what action the agent actually does perform, the agent, if she is to be considered responsible, must have been able to do otherwise. The present view, in contrast, denies that responsibility rests on the availability to the agent of at least two options. What matters is rather the availability of one very particular option, namely, the option to act in accordance with Reason.[2] If, on this view, the agent exercises this option, then it is irrelevant whether the agent might *not* have exercised it. In other words, it is irrelevant whether the agent had the ability to act in *dis*cordance with Reason. If, on the other hand, the agent does *not* exercise this option, then the question of whether she *could have* exercised it is all-important.

From one perspective, the difference between these two views may seem great. For on the Autonomy View, the ability necessary for responsibility is, as it were, bidirectional—it is an ability to do one thing *or* another, an ability to do X or something other than X. On the Reason View, in contrast, the ability necessary for responsibility is unidirectional—it is an ability to do one sort of thing, which is compatible with the *in*ability to do anything else.

From another perspective, however, the difference between these two views may seem very small. For with the exception of one very special type of case, the nominally different conditions of responsibility respectively entailed by the two views may be thought to amount to the same thing. Admittedly, regarding the case in which the agent actually does act in accordance with Reason—the case, that is, in which the agent does just what she ought to do for just the reasons that she ought to have—the Autonomy View requires that she have the ability to do otherwise while the Reason View does not. But when the agent fails to do what she ought to do, both views require that she could have done what she ought. And even when the agent does what she ought to do but not for the reasons that she ought to have, both views require that the agent could have acted in accordance with (and on the basis of) those reasons.

In other words, except in cases where the agent does the right thing for the right reasons, both views require that the responsible agent have the ability to do otherwise. Only in those cases in which the agent does do the right thing for the right reasons do the two views differ. And even there, it might be argued, the views differ in letter but not in spirit. For the spirit of the Autonomy View, it might be said, is to deny that responsibility is compatible with being fated to live one's life along a preordained track. The Autonomy View insists that the responsible agent be flexible, that she be able to choose and act in a way that is not forced upon her by the uncontrollable features and events of her past. But the Reason View might be thought to have the relevant kind of flexibility built into it. For the Reason View requires that the agent be able to act in accordance with Reason, and part of what it *is* to act in accordance with Reason is to be sensitive and responsive to relevant changes in one's situation and environment—that is, to be flexible (see Chapter 3, pp. 55–56).

Perhaps the proponent of the Autonomy View was a proponent of that view simply because she thought that the ability to do otherwise was necessary if an agent was to be sensitive and responsive to changes in the environment in rational ways. Perhaps she thought that if an agent could not act otherwise in a given situation, then it would have to be the case that the agent was acting blindly or rigidly, according to a rule that she was incapable of questioning. Perhaps it simply had not occurred to the proponent of autonomy that one explanation for why an agent might not be able to do otherwise is that it is so obviously rational to do what she plans to do and the agent is too rational to ignore that fact. Once this does occur to the proponent of autonomy, she may simply give up the Autonomy View and accept the Reason View as the view she was confusedly after all along.

Even if the Reason View may in this way appear as a mere refinement of the Autonomy View, the significance of the shift from autonomy to reason should not be underestimated. For the suggestion that autonomy is required for free will and responsibility involves the suggestion that the problems of free will and responsibility are, at the most fundamental level, purely metaphysical problems. The question we must answer, if we are to know whether we are free and responsible beings, concerns what metaphysical kinds of beings we are. In particular, we must know whether we are metaphysically integrated with other parts of nature; whether we are part of the same causal network as the rest of nature; whether we are subject, and wholly subject, to the same sorts of psychological and physical forces as other animals and things. If we are so subject, the Autonomy View suggests, that necessarily excludes us from the realm of free and responsible beings. For then our choices and the actions that flow from them are not ultimately up to us, but are rather consequences of the same combination of chance and determination that accounts for the flow of events that constitute the rest of the world. In order to be free and responsible beings, we must, on the contrary, be metaphysically distinctive, endowed with contracausal powers, or perhaps with our own peculiar and irreducible kind of causality.[3]

The Reason View locates the essence of the problems of free will and responsibility elsewhere. According to the Reason View, what we need to know if we are to find out whether we are free and responsible beings is whether we possess the ability to act in accordance with Reason. Since Reason is here understood to refer to the highest faculty or set of faculties there is, the faculty or set of faculties that, in most circumstances, will help us form true beliefs and good values, this amounts to the suggestion that we need to know whether we have the ability to think—and on the basis of our thought, to act—well rather than badly. That is, we need to know whether we have the ability to choose and to act on the basis of the right reasons for choosing and acting. And since we can assume that if one acts according to the right reasons one will perform the right action, the ability we are concerned with might be described as the ability to do the right thing for the right reasons. The question of whether we have this ability is not so much a metaphysical as a metaethical, and perhaps also an ethical, one. For we cannot answer it unless we know what counts as doing the right thing and having the right reasons.

To shift from the Autonomy View to the Reason View, then, is to shift from a view that takes the problems of responsibility and free will to be purely metaphysical problems, the solutions to which can be found independently of any metaethical commitments, to a view that takes these problems to be inextricably bound to metaethical, and perhaps also ethical, commitments. According to the Autonomy View, having the status of a responsible being depends on having a distinctive metaphysical power, the power to choose one path of action or another independently of any forces that would push one in one direction or the other. According to the Reason View, having responsible status depends rather on a distinctive intellectual power, the power to exercise right Reason and to govern one's actions accordingly. Since, again, right Reason refers to those faculties which will, in most circumstances, lead one to form true beliefs and good values, the power to exercise right Reason may be redescribed as the power to recognize the True and the Good. The ability to act in accordance with Reason might then be redescribed as the ability to act in accordance with, and on the basis of, the True and the Good.

If the Reason View is right, then proponents of autonomy are mistaken in regarding the problem of responsibility as a fundamentally metaphysical problem. They are mistaken in thinking that being responsible essentially requires being free of all external physical and psychological forces. But it is easy to see how the mistake could be made. For if the Reason View is right, then what responsibility really requires is the ability to act in accordance with and on the basis of the True and the Good, and it is easy to see how a person who is dimly in search of this ability might confusedly think that only beings who are free of all external physical or psychological forces could have it.

In particular, one can see how a person might think that if someone is governed by the True and the Good then she cannot be governed by one's garden variety of causes. To be governed by the True and the Good is not, after all, to be governed by the Past, and to do something because it is the right thing to do is not to do it because one has been taught to do it. One might think, then, that one can only be governed by one thing or the other. For if one is going to do whatever it is right to do, then it seems one will do it whether or not one has been so taught. And if one is going to do whatever one has been taught to do, then it seems one will do it whether or not it is right.

But such reasoning is mistaken. These two explanations do not compete, for they are explanations of different kinds. Perhaps an example or two will help to make this clear. Consider the following situation: You ask me to name the capital of Nevada, and I reply "Carson City." We can explain why I give this answer in either of the following ways: First, we can point out that when I was in the fifth grade I had to memorize the capitals of the states. I was taught to believe that Carson City was the capital of Nevada, and was subsequently positively reinforced for believing so. Second, we can point out that Carson City *is* the capital of Nevada, and that this was, after all, what you wanted to know. So, on the one hand, I gave my answer because I was taught. And, on the other, I gave my answer because it was right.

Presumably, these explanations are not unrelated. For if Carson City were not the capital of Nevada, I would not have been taught that it was. And if I hadn't been taught that Carson City was the capital of Nevada, I wouldn't have known that it was. Indeed, one might think that if the answer I gave weren't right, I *couldn't* have given it because I was taught. For no school board would have hired a teacher who got such facts wrong. And if I hadn't been taught that Carson City was the capital of Nevada, perhaps I couldn't have given this answer because it was right. For that Carson City is the capital of Nevada is not something that can be known *a priori*.

Similarly, we can explain why a person acts justly in either of the following ways: First, we can point out that she was taught to act justly, and was subsequently positively reinforced for doing so. Second, we can point out that it is right to act justly, and go on to say why she knows this is so. Again, these explanations are likely to be related. For it if weren't right to act justly, the person might well not have been taught that it was. And if the person hadn't been taught that she ought to act justly, the person might not have discovered this on her own. Of course, the explanations of both kinds in this case will be more complex than the explanations in the previous case. But what is relevant here is that these explanations are compatible: that one can be determined by the Good *and* determined by the Past.

The Reason View thus offers an explanation for the attractiveness of the Autonomy View: Once one sees what is really involved in being a free and responsible being—namely, having the ability to act in accordance with the True and the Good—then one can understand how it might have seemed that what was involved was a metaphysical property, namely, autonomy. For one can understand how having the ability to act in accordance with the True and the Good can seem to be incompatible with being metaphysically ordinary, with being subject, and wholly subject, to the same causal forces as those which govern the behavior of other animals and objects. Once we have identified the ability that this radical metaphysical independence seemed necessary to secure, however, we can see, first, that metaphysical independence is not necessary after all and, second, that we can state the condition of freedom and responsibility more directly by referring outright to the ability to act in accordance with (and on the basis of) the True and the Good.

The Reason View Compared with the Real Self View

In form, this response to autonomists is similar to a response that proponents of the Real Self View might make (and, indeed, it has something in common with Hume's own response, discussed in Chapter 2). For like the proponents of the Reason View, the proponents of the Real Self View believe they know what really matters for free will and responsibility. On their view, what really matters is the ability to act in accordance with one's valuational system, that is, the ability to act from one's Real Self. And though, they may point out, this ability may *seem* to require a peculiar metaphysical independence from causes (this suggestion was more fully elaborated in Chapter 3), on closer examination we can see that in fact no such metaphysical status is necessary.

Proponents of the Reason View and proponents of the Real Self View share the belief that the ability or freedom crucial to responsibility is unidirectional, that being responsible involves having the ability *to* act in one sort of way or on one sort of basis, but does not involve the ability *not* to act in that way or on that basis. Moreover, both views agree that having the requisite unidirectional ability is compatible with being metaphysically ordinary. Thus proponents of both views believe that, in cases in which agents seem not sufficiently free to be responsible, the problems lie not in whether but in how the actions of these agents are caused. To put it another way, they believe that the problems in these cases have to do not with the ultimacy but with the type of the agents' control of their behavior.

Just as other considerations promoted a perspective from which the difference between the Autonomy View and the Reason View seemed very slight, these considerations encourage us to see the Real Self View and the Reason View as very similar. For the Reason View and the Real Self View both suggest that what is of fundamental importance to freedom and responsibility is not the quantity but the quality of the option(s) available. These views differ simply with respect to *which* quality they take to be so important. According to the Real Self View, it is the ability to act in accordance with one's Real Self; according to the Reason View, it is the ability to act in accordance with Reason. But these two abilities may themselves be seen as very similar. For the Real Self View, by emphasizing the importance of the ability to act in accordance with one's values, stresses the fact that a responsible being must be able to choose her actions for herself, rather than let her actions be chosen for her by another person or even by a compulsive desire or habit with which she does not identify. The Reason View seems to make the same point—for, after all, the claim that a responsible being must be able to act in accordance with Reason is to be understood as insisting that the responsible being be able to act in accordance with *her own* Reason, that is, that she be able to exercise the faculties that will lead her to the True and the Good herself, and be able to govern her actions on that basis. Both views, then, seem primarily concerned to stress that a responsible being must be able to act on the basis of her own most deeply held thoughts and feelings. The Reason View is simply more restrictive than the Real Self View, insisting that the agent be able to identify her most deeply held thoughts and feelings with the thoughts and feelings that arise out of, or, at any rate, are capable of coexisting comfortably with, her exercise of Reason.

The way in which Reason is defined, however, makes this restriction more significant than it might at first seem, and thus makes the difference between the Reason View and the Real Self View considerable. For the difference between an agent who has the ability to act in accordance with Reason and an agent who lacks this ability is not essentially the difference between an agent who can form her values according to more intellectual, self-consciously deliberative means and an agent who forms her values in a less articulable and cognitive manner. Rather, the difference referred to is that between an agent who can form (and act on) right values because they are right—that is, an agent who is able to "track" the True and Good in her value judgments—and an agent who cannot.[4]

Thus, the difference between the Real Self View and the Reason View might be stated in the following way: According to the Real Self View, an individual is responsible if and only if she is able to form her actions on the basis of her values. The Reason View insists that responsibility requires something more. According to the Reason View, an individual is responsible if and only if she is able to form her actions on the basis of her values *and* she is able to form her values on the basis of what is True and Good.

Whether an agent is able to form her values on the basis of the True and the Good, however, is not solely a matter of the agent's intelligence, alertness, and psychological complexity. Two agents alike in these respects may nonetheless differ in their capacity to recognize the True and the Good. A victim of a deprived (or depraved) childhood, for example, may be as smart as a person raised in a more normal environment, but, because of a regrettably skewed set of experiences, her values may be distorted. She is able to reason, as it were, but not able to act in accordance with Reason. Having been exposed to an unfortuitous collection of data, *her* reason will not reach its goal.

This marks a fairly dramatic difference between the Reason View and the Real Self View. For where the Real Self View claims that the freedom to govern one's actions according to one's real self is all the freedom it is intelligible or at any rate necessary for a person to hope for, the Reason View insists that this is not enough. According to the Reason View, some real selves may be responsible while others may not, and individuals may be responsible for some actions that arise out of their real selves but not be responsible for others. In this respect, the Reason View is more like the Autonomy View. But we have already seen that while the Autonomy View takes the extra condition to be a purely metaphysical property, the property with which the Reason View is concerned is explicitly normative.

The Reason View as an Intermediary between the Other Views

In focusing on a feature of agents that is explicitly normative, the Reason View differs from both the Autonomy View and the Real Self View. For both these other views, the problems of free will and responsibility are understood to be purely metaphysical problems. The debate between the proponents of the last two views centers on the question of how much metaphysical freedom and power a responsible being is required to have. I have already mentioned that proponents of the Real Self View think that the freedom and power to govern one's actions according to one's real self are all the freedom and power it is intelligible or at any rate necessary for a person to hope for. Proponents of the Autonomy View claim that this is not sufficient. To be responsible, they say, an agent not only must be able to govern her actions by her real self, she also must be able to ensure that her real self is not in turn governed by anything else. Proponents of autonomy criticize their opponents for being unable to explain why being able to govern one's actions by one's real self should make a person responsible given that the person's real self may itself be the inevitable product of external forces. Proponents of the Real Self View question in return how it can make any difference whether the real self is an inevitable product of external forces or instead an arbitrary existent emerging inexplicably from the void.

From the perspective of the Reason View, both the criticisms these other views respectively level against the other are correct: The ability to act in accordance with one's real self is *not* sufficient to explain responsibility, but the real self's metaphysical independence from all other things will not explain it either. Both views, by searching for a property that can be stated in a way that is not implicitly value-laden, miss the crucial feature that distinguishes responsible beings from others.

This feature, according to the Reason View, is the ability to be in touch with the True and the Good. In other words, what makes responsible beings special is their ability to recognize good values as opposed to bad ones and to act in a way that expresses appreciation of this recognition. The freedom and power necessary for responsibility, then, are the freedom and power to *be* good, that is, the freedom and power to do the right thing for the right reasons. Having the ability to govern one's actions in accordance with one's real self does not necessarily guarantee this sort of freedom and power (remember the victim of the deprived childhood), but neither does the metaphysical independence of autonomous agency. Moreover, one may have this sort of freedom and power without metaphysical independence: One's ability to be good may *arise from* one's experiences; it need not exist *despite* them.

We might capture the difference between a nonresponsible being and a responsible one, then, by pointing out that the latter, unlike the former, is capable of recognizing things she might be responsible for. The responsible being is capable of recognizing that some actions, characters, and lives are better than others, of seeing which ones are better than others, and of controlling her behavior so as to make her actions, character, and life better rather than worse. That is why, if she does something good, she deserves a special kind of credit for it—the responsible being, and only the responsible being, knows what she is doing in the relevant sense, and does it on purpose. And that is why, if she does something wrong, she deserves a special kind of blame for it—the responsible being, and only the responsible being, could have and should have known better.

The proponents of the Autonomy View were right, then (and those of the Real Self View wrong), to insist that the ability to act in accordance with one's real self is insufficient for responsibility. The ability to ensure that one's actions are really one's own will not make one responsible unless one is oneself an appropriately special kind of being. The proponents of autonomy were wrong, though, (and those of the Real Self View right) to think that being appropriately special involves being metaphysically independent—that is, being ungoverned by anything else.

Certainly, there are some things that might govern a real self that would render it incapable of responsibility. But the problem is not *that* the real self is governed, but *by what*. A real self is incapable of responsibility if it is incapable of acting in accordance with and on the basis of the True and the Good, and this implies that a real self is incapable of responsibility if it is governed by something that prevents the agent from being able to recognize and appreciate the True and the Good. Presumably, certain traumatic experiences, bad role models, or neurological pathologies may exemplify such barriers to responsibility. But just as a real self is not responsible if it is governed by the wrong things, a real self is responsible if it is governed by the right, even if it is irresistibly governed by the right. For it may be that the reason one is able to recognize and appreciate the True and the Good is that one has been shaped, at the deepest level, by things that *make* one sensitive and responsive to good values. One has had a good moral education, perhaps, a good set of role models, and an environment that has developed in one dispositions of attention, sympathy, understanding, and sound reasoning.

In light of the above remarks, one might see the Reason View as an intermediary, though not a compromise, between the Real Self View and the Autonomy View. For the above remarks suggest a perspective from which the conditions of responsibility offered by the Real Self View are too weak, and from which the conditions offered by the Autonomy View are too strong. This shows itself in a somewhat startling way if one poses the question of how the Reason View compares to the other two alternatives with respect to the issue of whether responsibility is compatible with psychological determinism.

The Asymmetry of the Reason View

The Real Self View is naturally associated with compatibilism, for one may be determined to have a particular real self and one may be determined to act in accordance with it. From the point of view of a proponent of the Real Self View, then, the fact that an agent's action is determined is always compatible with her being responsible for it. The Autonomy View, on the other hand, is naturally associated with incompatibilism, for if one is determined to act in accordance with one's values, and one's values are determined by something external to oneself, then one's choices are not independent of external forces. From the point of view of a proponent of the Autonomy View, then, the fact that an agent's action is determined is always incompatible with her being responsible for it.

According to the Reason View, however, responsibility depends on the ability to act in accordance with the True and the Good. If one is psychologically determined to do the right thing for the right reasons, this is compatible with having the requisite ability. (Indeed, it would seem to be absolute proof that one has it.) But if one is psychologically determined to do the wrong thing, for whatever reason, this seems to constitute a denial of that ability. For if one *has* to do the wrong thing, then one *cannot* do the right, and so one lacks the ability to act in accordance with the True and the Good. The Reason View is thus committed to the curious claim that being psychologically determined to perform good actions is compatible with deserving praise for them, but that being psychologically determined to perform bad actions is not compatible with deserving blame.[5]

This claim sounds paradoxical so long as one continues to think of the problems of freedom and responsibility as purely metaphysical and nonnormative problems. For, metaphysically speaking, the person who is psychologically determined to perform a bad action may have no less control over her actions than the person who is psychologically determined to perform a good one, and the person who is determined to act rightly is no more free than the person who is determined to act wrongly. From a purely metaphysical perspective, then, it seems that either both determined agents must be responsible or neither can be. If the Reason View is right, however, then the purely metaphysical perspective common to the

Real Self View and the Autonomy View is mistaken. Though the two agents we are considering may have the same amount of freedom, they have freedom to do different things, and though the two agents may have the same degree of control, their control differs with respect to its value.

If we suspend our tendency to think of responsibility as a wholly metaphysical issue and examine our intuitions regarding particular cases, the air of paradox surrounding the asymmetry between good actions and bad ones disappears. For if phrases like "I couldn't help it," "he had no choice," "she couldn't resist" typically count as excuses intended to exempt the agent from blame for an action, they do not ordinarily serve as grounds for withholding praise. "I cannot tell a lie," "he couldn't hurt a fly" are not exemptions from praiseworthiness but testimonies to it. If a friend presents you with a gift and says she "couldn't resist," this suggests the strength of her friendship and not the weakness of her will. If one feels one "has no choice" but to speak out against injustice, one ought not to be upset about the depth of one's commitment. And one has reason to be grateful if, during times of trouble, one's family "cannot help" coming to one's aid.

Of course, these phrases must be given an appropriate interpretation if they are to indicate that the agent is deserving of praise. "He couldn't hurt a fly" must allude to someone's gentleness—it would be perverse to say this of someone who was in an iron lung. It is not admirable in George Washington that he cannot tell a lie, if it is because he has a tendency to stutter that inhibits his attempts. "He could not have done otherwise" as it is used in the context of praise, then, must be taken to imply something like "because he was too good." An action is praiseworthy only if it is done for the right reasons. So it must be only in light of and because of these reasons that the praiseworthy agent "could not help" doing the right thing.

If an agent "cannot help" doing the wrong thing, however, then the agent patently lacks the ability to do the right. Perhaps she can recognize the right thing but cannot execute it—consider the kleptomaniac who does not want to steal but must. Or perhaps she can perform whatever action she thinks right, but her judgments about what is right are inevitably incorrect. Again, we can consider the victim of the deprived childhood, but also the victim of deception, or even a person raised in a society in which false values are too effectively reinforced. Whatever the explanation that prevents the agent from being able to do the right thing for the right reasons, our intuitions seem to support the claim that the agent does not deserve blame. If an agent is incapable of doing the right thing for the right reasons, then it is not her fault that she stumbles into doing something wrong.

The Reason View Applied

Let us look more closely at the implications of the Reason View for specific cases. Let us see what the claim that an agent is responsible if and only if the agent can do the right thing for the right reasons entails.

We have already seen that it does not entail that the agent have the unconditional ability to do otherwise. For it is possible that the agent who can do the right thing for the right reasons cannot do anything *but* that. In particular, an agent's vision may be so clear that she cannot help seeing which action is "the right thing" and her virtue may be so sure that, knowing which action is right, she cannot help performing it. It is important to stress, though, that the agent who can do the right thing for the right reasons need not be like the agent just characterized. A person who does the right thing for the right reasons may be perfectly capable of doing something else. Moreover, an agent who actually does something else may yet have been capable of acting rightly. According to the Reason View, all three types of agents would be responsible beings, since it is only the ability to do the right thing for the right reasons, and not its inevitable exercise, that is required for responsibility.

With regard to agents who do the right thing and do so for the right reasons, then, the Reason View claims that it makes no difference whether they could have done anything else. In this respect, the Reason View is different from and more plausible than the Autonomy View. To see this, recall the lifesaver cases discussed in Chapter 3: Two persons, of equal swimming ability, stand on equally uncrowded beaches. Each sees an unknown child struggling in the water in the distance. Each thinks "The child needs my help" and directly swims out to save him. In each case, we assume that the agent reasons correctly—the child *does* need her help—and that, in swimming out to save him, the agent does the right thing. We further assume that in one of these cases, the agent has the ability to do otherwise, and in the other case not. According to the Autonomy View, only the first of these agents is then responsible. But it may be that the second agent lacks the ability to do otherwise simply because her understanding of the situation is so good and her moral commitment so strong. And even if this is not the explanation—if, in particular, the difference between the two agents is a metaphysical fact with no psychological implications—this hardly seems grounds for withholding praise from the second agent while giving it to the first. For there seems to be nothing of value that the first agent has but the second agent lacks. Both examples are examples of agents' thinking and doing exactly what we want agents to think and to do. Just as it would be absurd for the strength of one's commitment to exclude one from praiseworthiness, so would it be absurd to insist, for example, that one's moral character be perfect. Neither the fact that one is determined to do the right thing for the right reasons nor the fact that one is not so determined make one any less praiseworthy, so long as one actually does the right thing, and does it for the right reasons.

We must remember, however, that "doing the right thing for the right reasons" names a much narrower category than simply "doing the right thing." Only if a person acts for the right reasons does she deserve praise, and only if she is capable of so acting is she a responsible being. We all have our favorite examples of the person who helps others out of self-interested motives—the shopkeeper who gives children correct change because the policy is good for business, the philanthropist who gives away millions in order to impress her friends or to write it off on her taxes. But for the purpose of understanding the problem of responsibility, it is more illuminating to focus on a gap between "doing the right thing" and "doing it for the right reasons" that is less commonly noticed. In addition to the contrast between the agent who acts out of unselfish or moral motives and the agent who acts out of selfish or amoral ones, we should attend to the difference between the agent who is governed by intelligent and perceptive reasons and the agent who is governed by unintelligent or neurotic ones.

A person may, for example, act according to a good moral precept without ever having stopped to think whether or why it is good. Much of the time we simply do whatever our family or friends do, whatever our society encourages. If our familial and social circles happen to have good patterns of behavior, then our behavior will be good as well. We do the right thing, in these cases, not for the wrong reasons, but not for the right reasons either. Rather, we do it unthinkingly, blindly, by rote.

A different sort of case arises when a person's appreciation of one virtue is out of proportion to her appreciation of others. A person can get "hung up" on honesty, or be obsessed by the need to be generous or courageous. People sometimes take the value of loyalty too far; others, focusing too narrowly on the importance of impartiality, may not take loyalty far enough. When a person's devotion to a virtue is obsessive, her exhibitions of that virtue may not deserve praise. Thus, we may distinguish between a healthy form of patriotism and an unhealthy one. Either form may motivate the same desirable act, but we may think that the healthy patriot acts for the right reason and that the unhealthy patriot does not.

The importance of emphasizing the narrow scope of doing the right thing for the right reasons lies not in preventing the possibility of being too generous with one's praise but in avoiding the danger of being too lenient about the conditions of responsibility. For, according to the Reason View, the agent who does the right thing for the right reasons is responsible even if she cannot help doing that. It is important to see, then, that the person who cannot help doing the right thing for the right reasons is not the same person as the one who cannot help doing the right thing because everyone else in her society does it, nor is she the same as the person who cannot help doing the right thing because she has some sort of morality complex.

To return to examples, let us consider the woman who buys a gift for her friend claiming that she could not resist. Walking past a shop window, she sees a book that she knows her friend has been searching for for ages. It is only ten dollars, and so, imagining the delight on her friend's face when she delivers the book, she walks into the shop and buys it. Now there is nothing in this story that tells us whether the woman could have refrained from buying the book, and when she says to her friend, "I couldn't resist," there is no reason to think that she means this phrase literally. After all, the woman didn't *try* to resist—how should she know whether she could have? Still, according to the Reason View, even if the woman's remark, taken literally, were true, this would not prevent her from being a responsible agent. Assuming that she did the right thing for the right reasons (in this case, it would be more natural to say "assuming that she acted well, on noble motives"), the woman was responsible, and so deserves praise for her act of generosity whether she literally could have resisted performing it or not.

But to assume that she did the right thing for the right reasons is to assume quite a lot. It implies not only that she acted for her friend's sake and not for her own but also that her interest in her friend was healthy and in sound proportion to her interest in other people and things. In this context, the claim that the woman could not resist does not mean that the woman would have bought her friend the book no matter how much it cost or no matter how much she may have needed the money for other purposes. The assumption that she acted for the right reasons actually excludes these possibilities, for it implies that she acted out of a reasonable and desirable generosity and not out of an obsessive or foolish one. The claim that the agent could not have helped doing the right thing for the right reasons, then, actually implies that if the situation had been relevantly different, the agent could have done something else.

According to the Reason View, the praiseworthiness of the agent depends on her doing the right thing, and on her doing it for the right reasons. In other words, her praiseworthiness depends on her act's being an exhibition of her ability to govern her actions in accordance with the True and the Good. Moreover, this is all her praiseworthiness depends on. Once we know that her act was one of admirable generosity in the context of a healthy and rewarding form of friendship, we know all we need to know to justify our praise. The answer to the question of whether she could have been a less generous friend simply does not matter.

If, on the other hand, the woman had not bought the book and had thus acted in a disappointingly ungenerous manner, then the question of whether she could have been a more generous friend would matter. For it may be that the woman was twenty minutes late for an important appointment at the time she passed the bookstore. Or perhaps she was too distracted by thoughts of her job or her children or the Middle East situation to notice the titles of books in the shop window. Less obviously, she may have been able to notice the titles of books, but her preoccupations may have prevented her from connecting the relevant title with her friend. If, for any of these reasons, the woman could not have performed the generous act, then she may not be responsible for her failure.

Blameworthiness According to the Reason View

So far the implications of the Reason View for specific cases seem to match the conclusion of the Real Self View. For whenever the agent is able to do the right thing for the right reasons, she is also able to act in accordance with her values, and so express her real self. (If she has the right reasons, they are presumed to be among her values.) And the examples above would suggest that whenever an agent is not able to do the right thing for the right reasons, she is also not able to act in accordance with her values. Another example, however, will bring out the difference between the Reason View and the Real Self View.

Imagine that the woman did not and could not have stopped to buy the book for her friend, but that the explanation for this does not lie in the distractions or the demands of her immediate circumstances. Rather, imagine that the explanation has to do with the woman's personality and the history of her social development. Perhaps she is too self-centered for the thought "My friend would like this book" to occur to her, or perhaps she is so unfamiliar with examples of sincere, noninstrumental friendships that the thought "I should buy this book, just to make my friend happy" cannot help appearing irrational to her. Assuming that the person does not mind being the kind of person she is—she thinks it is quite a reasonable, perhaps the only reasonable way to be—then, in not buying the book, she acts in accordance with her values and expresses her real self. According to the Real Self View, this person is responsible for her failure in friendship. According to the Reason View, however, she is not. For by hypothesis the person in question is *unable* to have different and better values—she is unable to change her real self in accordance with the True and the Good. With respect to the difference between the Real Self View and the Reason View in this case, the Reason View seems more plausible. For what we are here imagining is a person incapable of friendship, and it seems obvious that a person incapable of friendship is to be pitied rather than blamed.

Of course, the question of whether a person is truly incapable of friendship, or, for that matter, incapable of good temper, punctuality, or any other socially desirable trait, is apt to be controversial. The fact that a person *is* consistently self-centered does not imply that she *has* to be. Yet, according to the Reason View, an agent's responsibility turns on the truth or falsity of the latter claim. A person who acts badly, whether routinely or in an individual case, deserves blame for doing so if that person is capable of understanding that she acts badly and is able to use this understanding to act differently. A person who acts badly does not deserve blame if she is not in a position to understand that her action is bad, or if, understanding it to be bad, she remains unable to govern her actions accordingly. But it is hard to know whether a person who acts badly could have acted less badly, particularly if her action fits a consistent pattern of behavior. How are we to decide whether a person regularly fails to exercise an ability to reason and act better than she does or whether she simply lacks the ability altogether?

Typically, we base such decisions on evidence involving a more thorough knowledge of the individual or on comparisons between that individual and others who seem relevantly similar. If persons with a similar history all fail to develop a particular desirable trait, we tend to conclude that their history renders them incapable of developing it. If, on the other hand, some persons develop well while others develop badly and no apparently relevant differences are found in the heredities and environments of the two groups, then we are likely to conclude that the persons in question all have the ability to act well, but that some of them exercise this ability and others do not.

It is misleading to speak as if our judgments about persons' abilities to do things are an all-or-nothing matter. We are more likely to judge that it would be very unlikely for a person of a certain background to develop a certain trait than we are to judge that it would be literally impossible for that to happen. Though one may interpret this to mean that it is statistically improbable that such a person will have the all-or-nothing ability to develop that way, more often, I think, it expresses the view that it would be difficult for such a person to develop that way. We might even say that such a person is *less* able to develop that way than others, meaning that it would take more ingenuity or effort on her part. It is not unnatural that we make such judgments, given the statistical nature of our evidence. Since a larger percentage of people quit smoking than break heroin addictions, we conclude that heroin addiction is stronger, that is, more difficult to break, than nicotine addiction. Accordingly, we blame smokers for continuing to smoke (insofar as we are inclined to blame them) more strongly than we blame heroin addicts for continuing to be addicts.

The Reason View can easily accommodate the notion that ability is a matter of degree. If we think that some people are less able than others to act in accordance with the True and the Good, then the Reason View allows, as do our intuitions, that they will be less responsible, and so less blameworthy for failing to so act. It may be pointed out, however, that our evidence for these judgments if far from perfect. Most of the time we judge whether persons are able to do things on the basis of very small and unscientific comparative samples. And even if we observed a large number of people with similar backgrounds none of whom exhibited a particular character trait, this would not prove beyond a shadow of a doubt that they were all unable to develop that trait. Conversely, even if nine people out of ten quit smoking when they embarked on a particular program, that would not prove that the remaining ten percent could have stopped smoking but didn't. The conclusion to be drawn from this is that many of the judgments we make about whether people could have done things that they failed to do are uncertain, and so attributions about responsibility that rely on such judgments must be uncertain as well. Since, according to the Reason View, responsibility for bad action does depend on such judgments, the Reason View implies that we are not always in a position to know whether an agent is responsible and blameworthy. But this does not detract from the Reason View, for the view does not attempt to provide us with a way of knowing whether a person is responsible for an act. It only tells us what we would need to know if we wanted to discover this fact.

What we need to know in general is, to repeat, that the agent is able to do the right thing for the right reasons, that is, that the agent is able to act in accordance with the True and the Good. This ability may be roughly analyzed into two narrower abilities. The first is an ability of thought, the ability to *know* what is in accordance with the True and the Good; the second is an ability of execution, the ability to convert one's knowledge into action. With respect to a bad-acting agent, then, we need to know whether she could have known better and whether, knowing better, she could have acted better. The bad-acting agent, if she is responsible, must have been *able* to do both these things. Since she failed to do at least one of them, she must be guilty of at least one of two types of moral failure.

A person who is able to know, but fails to know, what is in accordance with the True and the Good is guilty of a kind of negligence, a certain laziness of the mind. A person who fails to ask herself whether it is all right to work for a nuclear arms manufacturer or who simply does not think about whether a portion of her salary ought to be given to charity might exemplify a failure of this kind. Exhibitions of thoughtlessness, carelessness, or inconsiderate behavior might also be forms of this type of fault. One simply forgets one's grandmother's birthday. The thought that at this time of night one's upstairs neighbors might be disturbed by the volume of one's stereo just does not cross one's mind. These failures are culpable only if the agents in question did not have to fail—if the agents, in other words, could have raised the right questions and could have come to the right conclusions, if they could have had the thoughts that they did not actually have. But given certain assumptions about the agents' cognitive abilities, past experiences, and present circumstances, this conclusion does not seem unreasonable. Consider, for example, a person of average intelligence and perceptiveness, who has been exposed to moral questioning and argument, and who occasionally receives solicitations from Oxfam, Amnesty International, and the like. Assuming that she is not overwhelmed by personal troubles, that she is not misinformed about these organizations' effectiveness, and so on, what reason is there to think that the person is not able to raise the question of charity on her own?[6]

Just as a person may be capable of knowing the right thing to do but fail to know it nonetheless, a person who knows the right thing to do may be capable of doing it but fail to do it nonetheless. This would be a failure of execution that is a form of weakness of the will. It is as easy to imagine this type of failure as it is to imagine the former type. One knows that one ought to visit one's friend in the hospital, but one goes to the movies instead. One knows that one ought to point out that the waitress has undercharged one, but it is easy to be silent and pay the smaller bill. Again, the agents in question will be culpable only if they could have acted on their knowledge. But again, assuming that transportation to the hospital is no less convenient than transportation to the movies, that the diner is not mute nor the waitress deaf, that neither agent is driven by neurotic compulsion or dire need—what reason is there for thinking that the agents could not have acted as they knew best?

Philosophical questions remain about the justification and meaning of the claim that an agent who actually does one thing could unconditionally be doing another. Some of these questions will be pursued in the next chapter. In ordinary discourse, however, we make and assume claims of this sort all the time, and it does not seem implausible that our judgments about responsibility should rely on them.

The Unity and Spirit of the Reason View

According to the Reason View, our judgments about the responsibility of bad-acting agents do rely on claims of this sort. In this respect, I have argued, the Reason View is more plausible than the Real Self View. But the Reason View also denies that judgments about the responsibility of good-acting agents rely on claims of this sort. In this respect, I have argued, the Reason View is more plausible than the Autonomy View. Our intuitions about blame, both in general and with respect to individual cases, accord better with the Reason View than with the Real Self View. Our intuitions about praise, both in general and with respect to individual cases, accord better with the Reason View than with the Autonomy View. Thus, the Reason View seems to accord with and account for the whole set of our intuitions about responsibility better than either of the leading alternatives.

To draw this conclusion from these premises, however, is open to objection. For this inference assumes that the whole set of our intuitions about responsibility consists in the union of our intuitions about praise and our intuitions about blame. Against this assumption, it may be pointed out first that we think of responsibility as more unified than that—we understand responsibility to be a single feature of agents that makes them suitable objects of *either* praise or blame. Second, it may be noted that our concern with the issue of responsibility is not wholly tied to its connection with praise and blame. Our lives are not exclusively devoted to amassing credit and avoiding discredit, after all, and the goal of trying to make something of oneself, or even of trying to live above reproach, is hardly the highest goal on everyone's list. Though some people may want to be free and responsible beings because they want to be subject to deep evaluations, others may care about freedom and responsibility for what seem to be totally independent reasons. In particular, some may be concerned simply with their ability to govern their own actions, their ability to choose for themselves what to be and how to live. When we concentrate on this aspect of our interest in freedom and responsibility, the Reason View, with its emphasis on our connection to the True and the Good, may seem beside the point.

A further examination of the Reason View, however, yields answers to these objections. To the first objection, that the Reason View offers a segmented rather than a unified account of the concept of responsibility, we may reply that the appearance of disunity is an illusion, generated by the persistent tendency to see the problem of responsibility in fundamentally metaphysical terms and by the need to defend the view by comparing it to alternatives that encourage this tendency. From this purely metaphysical perspective, one may get the impression that the Reason View offers one set of conditions for being responsible for a good or desirable act and another set of conditions for being responsible for a bad or undesirable one. But in fact the Reason View proposes a single set of conditions for responsibility for any type of act: namely, that, at the time of performance, the agent possesses the ability to act in accordance with the True and the Good.[7] Whether the agent has this ability, and so whether the agent is responsible, is presumably independent of and prior to the question of whether she exercises it. The possession of this single and unified ability, then, underlies the agent's susceptibility to either praise or blame. If she deserves praise, it is for the exercise of her ability to act in accordance with the True and the Good. If she deserves blame, it is for the fact that she acted badly despite her ability to know and to do something better.

Indeed, the ability to act in accordance with the True and the Good is one the agent can be said to have or to lack at any time, including those times when the agent is doing nothing that one would want either to praise or to blame. Thus, the question of whether an agent is responsible for her actions can be answered even when the justification of praise or blame is not at issue. This is as it should be, since much of the time our actions are neither good nor bad and yet it seems intelligible to wonder whether we are responsible for them. I might wonder, for example, whether it is really up to me, in the relevant sense, to drink coffee, to exhibit a fondness for purple, to spend so much time doing philosophy. According to the Reason View, it is up to me if my decisions to do these things are made in the light of my knowledge or of my access to knowledge of the (true and good) reasons for doing and not doing them (assuming as well that my doing these things is dependent on my decisions to do them). For example, I am responsible for drinking coffee if in deciding whether to drink it, I am in a position to know, appreciate, and act on the reasons for and against drinking it. If, on the other hand, I am not in such a position—if perhaps I am hypnotized to drink coffee, or deceived about what is in my cup—then I am not responsible for drinking it.

This still leaves the second objection, however; that the conception of responsibility implicit in the Reason View is too exclusively tied to the issue of susceptibility to praise and blame to explain the various types of importance our status as responsible beings may have for us. According to the Reason View, being responsible consists in being able to act in accordance with Reason, that is, in being able to do the right thing for the right reasons, that is, in being able to be and do good. But if that were what responsibility consisted in, the objection goes, it would seem that our only reason for caring about responsibility would be that we care more fundamentally about being rational and good. In fact, however, there are many people who do not care (much) about being rational and good, who, it is intelligible to suppose, may still care about being responsible beings. They may not care about whether their lives are good or bad or whether their conduct deserves praise or blame and yet be concerned that, whatever their lives are, they are that way by their own choice. It is not obvious that the ability to act in accordance with the True and the Good is necessary in order for one's life to be governable by one's choice. Indeed, it is not obvious that these two properties are even related.

But they *are* related. For when one speaks of the desire to make one's own choice, one implicitly assumes that one knows what one is choosing between. If people had to select their spouses or careers by picking names out of a hat, it would be a cruel joke to say they were choosing them for themselves. One wants to choose with one's eyes open, so to speak. Choosing blindly would not satisfy one's desire at all. In other words, one wants to be able to choose in light of the knowledge of one's options and in light of the comparative reasons for and against these options. To want this, however, is just to want to choose in light of the True and the Good.

It may be noted that wanting to choose *in light of* the True and the Good does not commit one to wanting to choose *in accordance with* the True and the Good. One might, I suppose, fully recognize that one action would be better and yet choose to perform another. But even if a person did not want or care about acting in accordance with the True and the Good, she would still have to want the ability to so act if she cared about governing her own actions. For, as mentioned earlier, the ability to act in accordance with the True and the Good is composed of the ability to know the True and the Good, that is, to form one's values and plans in light of them, and the ability to convert one's values and plans into action. If one lacked the first component, the choices one made would be blind. If one lacked the second, one's choices would be ineffective.

One might initially attempt to describe the freedom necessary for responsibility as the freedom to do whatever one wants or, alternatively, as the freedom to do whatever one chooses. When it is pointed out that this allows the possibility that one's wants or choices be themselves externally determined, one may revise one's original description by adding that one also needs the freedom to want whatever one wants to want[8] or, alternatively, the freedom to choose whatever one chooses to choose. Clearly, this attempt at revision will only lead to an infinitely embedded condition that cannot ultimately succeed. Yet some revision is certainly necessary. Implicit in the Reason View is the recognition that the freedom that is necessary in addition to the freedom to do whatever one wants or chooses is the freedom that one's wants and choices be freely formed, formed, that is, in the absence of delusion and compulsion, and in the presence of Reason and (metaphorical) light. The freedom necessary for responsibility, then, is not just the freedom that allows one's actions to be governed by one's reasons, but also a freedom that allows one's reasons to be governed by what reasons there are.

Our desire to be responsible for our actions is a desire for our actions to be our own, for our responses to the world to be of our own making. It is not, however, a desire that the world itself be of our own making. The freedom necessary for responsibility is a freedom *within* the world, not a freedom *from* it. The Reason View recognizes that freedom within the world requires the ability to see and appreciate the world for what it is.

5

Ability and Possibility

(In Which the Implications of Determinism
for Responsibility Are Discussed)

According to the Reason View, the freedom necessary for responsibility consists in the ability (or freedom) to do the right thing for the right reasons—or, as I have sometimes put it, the ability (or freedom) to choose and to act in accordance with the True and the Good. By now, I hope I have said enough in defense and explanation of this view to make its main features both comprehensible and plausible. Still, in developing and presenting this view, I have had to rely on a common understanding and acceptance of concepts and ideas that are themselves philosophically problematic, or, at any rate, controversial. Any effort to get a more concrete and precise conception of responsibility, to fill in the outlines of the Reason View as it has so far been sketched, requires a closer examination of these concepts and the uses to which they have been put.

Two notions, in particular, will arouse philosophical concern. First, because the Reason View regards an agent's status as a responsible being as a matter of her possession of certain abilities, and, especially, certain psychological abilities, it will be important to understand what a psychological ability is. More specifically, it will be important to know what, if any, metaphysical conditions must be satisfied in order for attributions of psychological abilities to agents ever to be justified. Second, because the abilities the Reason View requires most notably include the ability to see and appreciate the True and the Good, it will be important to understand what "the True and the Good" can possibly refer to if they are to be the sorts of things that can be seen and appreciated in the requisite way. In particular, it will be important to understand and evaluate the metaethical assumptions that are necessary to make the Reason View coherent.

In this chapter and the succeeding one, I shall take up these two problems respectively. But it should be noted that the first cannot be discussed without involving one directly in the mind-body problem and that the second is inseparable from the general issue of the objectivity of values. Since these issues are arguably as complicated, as difficult, and as deep as the problems of responsibility and free will themselves, the remarks I am able to make about them here will inevitably be sketchy and incomplete. Moreover, although I shall present my views on these matters and my reasons for them as convincingly as possible, I am more tentative about them than I am about the approach to the problem of responsibility that has been presented in the earlier chapters.

In any event, it seems to me that the interest of the Reason View as an approach to responsibility should not be too tightly tied to the persuasiveness and plausibility of the arguments and views that follow. For although *some* answers to the questions these chapters take up are undeniably necessary in order for the Reason View to be more completely determinate and more thoroughly intelligible, these answers might be better supplied or supported by philosophers other than myself. And, indeed, even if it were to be ultimately decided that correct views about the mind-body problem or about the objectivity of values make the concept of responsibility incoherent or unrealizable, this would not wholly deprive the Reason View of interest. For, in that case, although the Reason View would not be able to achieve its goal of outlining how and when we can be responsible agents, it might still be valuable in explaining why we can never be.

With these qualifying remarks out of the way, let us turn to the first of the two issues that remain to be discussed, namely, that of

understanding what psychological abilities are and what metaphysical theses are compatible with their possession.

Determinism and the Reason View

It is a familiar fact that the status of responsibility is felt by many to
be threatened by determinism. In Chapters 1 and 2, I suggested that
much of the time this is due to the (perhaps unformulated) belief
that responsibility requires autonomy and that autonomy is threatened by determinism. But, as I argued in Chapters 3 and 4, the
belief that autonomy is required for responsibility is mistaken.
Once we have seen that autonomy, strictly speaking, involves the
ability to choose and to act independently of all, even all rational,
bases, we see that responsibility requires something more limited
than that, namely, the ability to choose and to act in accordance
with Reason, that is, the ability to choose and to act in accordance
with what reasons there are.

If the previous chapters of this book have been at all convincing,
then the path that leads people to incompatibilism by way of the
idea of autonomy can now be closed. Indeed, it may seem that all
paths to incompatibilism may now be closed. For it seems compatible with a person's being *able* to choose and to act in accordance
with Reason that she be determined to do so, and so the answer to
the question "Is determinism compatible with responsibility?"
would seem at least sometimes to be yes.

The fact that some responsible actions might be fully determined
does not, however, directly imply that responsibility is compatible
with determinism. For determinism is a general thesis that states
that all actions (or all events) are determined, and it is possible that
an essentially nondeterminist background is necessary in order for
individual determined actions to be ones for which their agents are
responsible. This would be the case, for example, if an essentially
nondeterminist background were required in order for some events
to be reasonably interpreted as *actions* at all.

Moreover, the basis for rejecting incompatibilism that we are
now considering would at best support the compatibility of determinism with some good, or at least rationally endorsable, actions,
and the idea that, if determinism is true, people are sometimes

responsible for good and rational actions but never responsible for bad and irrational ones is surprising and counterintuitive enough to make one suspicious. If the Reason View implied that conclusion, that would not constitute a refutation of it. Still, the conclusion would be very hard to swallow, and might well make one wonder whether our ordinary notion of responsibility were still being discussed.

In order to determine what metaphysical conclusions are implied by the Reason View, we need to better understand the notion of ability on which that view relies. Since the Reason View analyzes responsibility in terms of the possession of certain abilities, the question of what the metaphysical requirements of responsibility are boils down to the question of what metaphysical conditions are compatible with their possession.

The difficulty of this question can immediately be seen if we focus on a case in which these abilities are not exercised. When a person does not do the right thing for the right reasons, what does it mean to say that she could have done it? It is natural to think that, at the least, it implies that it was possible for her to do it, and this suggests that having the ability to do something that one does not actually do is directly incompatible with determinism. On the other hand, the *mere* possibility that one do a certain thing does not seem sufficient for the attribution of an ability either. It is possible that I may trip on my walk to work this morning, for example, but that does not mean that I have an *ability* to trip. So my having an ability to do something seems to involve more than the mere possibility that I do it. What?

Conditional Analyses of Ability

One proposal, prominently supported by G. E. Moore, analyzes "ability" as a conditional. According to Moore, "A could have done X" means "A would have done X, *if* A had chosen." This proposal nicely captures the thought that the difference between your having the ability to do something and its merely being possible that you do it lies in the fact that, in the former case, you can make it happen (that you do it) if you want to. Moreover, this proposal has the advantage of making unexercised abilities compatible with determinism after all. But a number of problems with this, and indeed with any, conditional analysis of ability have been pointed out that, to my mind at least, have decisively defeated this approach.

Before describing these problems, it will be helpful to note that the conditions for attributing abilities to people vary considerably according to context. The question "Is A able to X?" will be a request for different information depending on the interests on behalf of which the question is asked. Moreover, in ordinary language there may be subtle differences in the use of "is able to," "has the ability to," and, more simply, "can." For present purposes, these differences shall be ignored and the expressions shall be used interchangeably. But it is extremely important that the *context* of the discussion be kept in mind. Specifically, our interest is in understanding what is involved in attributing to someone the ability to do something insofar as it is or may be relevant to assessing her responsibility for doing or not doing it.

The importance of keeping this context in mind can be illustrated in connection with our discussion of the merits and demerits of Moore's analysis, for it bears on the objection to this analysis, introduced by Roderick Chisholm, that has received the most attention in recent literature. Specifically, Chisholm noted that its being true that "A would have done otherwise *if* A had chosen," is compatible with its being the case that A *could not have chosen* to do otherwise. In such a case, Chisholm claims, A could not have done otherwise after all. Since our interest is restricted to the sense of "could have" that is relevant to assessments of responsibility, however, doubts may be raised as to the relevance of Chisholm's point. For consider the case of a man who, having been offered fifty dollars for the time of day, is thereby determined to give it to the woman who made the offer. He very probably would have told her the time for free, but, with the added incentive, he is absolutely determined to do so. In such a case, though we may grant Chisholm a sense in which the man could not have chosen to keep silent and so could not have done so, it is hard to see why this should deprive him of responsibility for the choice he did make (and the action he performed). What seems relevant to responsibility here is that his action followed from and was dependent on his choice, and this seems sufficiently reflected by the acknowledgment that he would have acted otherwise if he had chosen.

Nonetheless, there are other cases in which Chisholm's objection seems directly to the point. Thus, the fact that a person attacked on a dark street would have screamed if she had chosen cannot possibly support a positive evaluation of her responsibility in the case if she was too paralyzed by fear to consider, much less choose, whether to scream. Since one counterexample is enough to refute a given proposal, Chisholm's objection to Moore's analysis ultimately stands.

Conditional analyses of "could have done otherwise" face other problems as well: If we understand the analysans as a strict logical conditional, we can easily construct examples in which the conditional is true but the analysandum false. Some of these cases will be ones in which "If A chooses to X, A will X" because A will X whether A chooses to or not. Thus, the fact that my skin turns red in the sun does not mean that I am able to turn my skin red in the sun; that I am five feet two inches tall does not mean that I am able to be five foot two. Another set of cases are those in which, as a matter of fact, A *never* chooses to X. The fact that I will never choose to go hang-gliding means that, in a strict sense, the relevant conditional is true. But clearly that does not justify the claim that I am able to hang-glide.

One might think that this problem could be solved by interpreting the conditional in a more natural way, thereby expressing a tighter connection between A's choosing to X and A's X-ing. For example, one might interpret "A would have done X, if A had chosen" to mean "If A chooses to X, A will X, and if A doesn't choose to X, A will not X." But this makes the connection between A's choice to X and A's X-ing too strong, falsely suggesting that a person has an ability to do something only if she can do it (or not) at will. That a person has the ability to understand English does not imply that she also has an ability not to understand it. That a person is able to discriminate red from green does not imply that she can also not discriminate.

At least as important (and as puzzling) as these cases are those in which the analysandum seems true and the analysans false. A perfect example is provided by J. L. Austin in a footnote to "Ifs and Cans":

> Consider the case where I miss a very short putt and kick myself because I could have holed it. It is not that I should have holed it if I had tried: I did try, and missed. It is not that I should have holed it if

conditions had been different: that might of course be so, but I am talking about conditions as they precisely were, and asserting that I could have holed it. There is the rub.[1]

Austin goes on to note that if determinism is true, such assertions may always be false. That is, it may follow from determinism that nobody ever could have done anything she did not actually do. His point, however, is not about the truth of such assertions but about their meaning. His point is that, at least sometimes, when someone. says that she could have done otherwise, she is not saying that she would have done otherwise, if some condition or other had been different—she is saying that she could have done otherwise, *given conditions precisely as they were.*

Since conditional analyses of "could have done otherwise" lend support to compatibilist accounts of free will, the rejection of such analyses has typically been associated with incompatibilism. Indeed, if we focus on the sort of example Austin gives us, this connection seems all but unavoidable. For, as we have noted, this type of example stresses the fact that, in at least some contexts, the assertion that A could have done otherwise does not mean that A would have done otherwise *if* some condition or other had been different—it means (unanalyzably, it would seem) that A *could* have done otherwise *given conditions precisely as they were.* It is hard to resist the thought that in order for this assertion to be true, it must at the very least have been *possible* for A to do otherwise— and not just logically possible or epistemologically possible either, but physically, psychologically, *substantively* possible that A do otherwise given conditions precisely as they were. Since determinism seems automatically to rule out the substantive possibility that A have done otherwise, the rejection of conditional analyses of the ability to do otherwise seems to lead us straightway to incompatibilism.

An Alternative Characterization of Ability

If this reasoning were correct, then determinism would imply that no one is ever able to do what she in fact fails to do. In particular, it would imply that anyone who fails to do the right thing for the right reason is also unable to do it. In conjunction with the Reason View, then, determinism would imply that no one is ever responsible for acting wrongly. However, I believe the reasoning that leads to this conclusion is incorrect.

Rather, different kinds of determinism seem to me to have different implications for the attribution of abilities, keeping in mind the restriction that the attributions in question are such as may be relevant to an assessment of responsibility. Let me characterize psychological determinism, roughly, as the thesis that all psychological events are uniquely and wholly determined by a conjunction of laws and states of affairs that are capable of description at the psychological level of explanation. Then psychological determinism does seem to me incompatible with responsibility, at least for wrong actions. But the thesis of psychological determinism has virtually nothing to support it. Other forms of determinism, on the other hand, which may be empirically more plausible, seem to me to have no clear implications for the attributions of ability in question.

Although I can offer no reductive analysis of "ability," of the sort that Moore tried to produce, and from which these compatibilist conclusions could be securely derived, I can give a *characterization* of what is involved in attributing an ability to someone, which will at least allow me to explain why the thesis of determinism *per se* seems irrelevant to it. In particular, we may characterize the attribution of the ability to X as consisting of two claims, one positive and one negative. The positive claim is that the individual to whom the ability is attributed possesses whatever capacities, skills, talents, knowledge, and so on are necessary for X-ing. Thus, for example, the ability to walk requires that one's legs and the relevant parts of one's brain and nervous system are functioning properly and that one has learned how to walk. The negative claim is that nothing interferes with or prevents the exercise of the relevant capacities, skills, talents, and so on. Thus, for example, one is not able to walk if one's legs are bound to a chair.

In light of this characterization, the claim that A is unable to X can be understood as the claim that either A lacks at least one of the capacities, talents, skills or whatever that are necessary for X-ing or something prevents or interferes with A's exercise of these capacities, talents, or skills. Wanting to know whether being determined not to X renders one unable to X—or, more precisely, wanting to know whether being determined not to X implies that something renders one unable to X—is, then, a matter of wanting to know whether being determined not to X implies either of the disjuncts above.

It seems very unlikely that determinism should imply that the first disjunct is always satisfied. For it is hard to imagine how, for example, my being determined to remain seated during a lecture should imply that I lack the capacities, skills, and knowledge necessary for walking. It seems vastly implausible that every time I am determined to be still, I am also unconsciously stricken by paralysis or something of that sort, and it seems wholly gratuitous to suppose that determinism should have such a consequence.

It is less obvious that determinism lacks a connection to the truth or falsity of the second disjunct. For although the suggestion that every time one is determined to be still, one's legs are invisibly bound (or something of that sort) is absurd, there may yet be subtle and unobserved events that prevent us from walking, and the suggestion that determinism might imply the existence of such events (whenever we do not walk) may be less obviously false. Our concern, however, is whether determinism *must* imply this result, whether, that is, the truth of determinism *per se* is sufficient to establish this conclusion. We need to know, that is, whether the mere fact that one is determined not to X implies that something actually prevents or interferes with one's X-ing, or with one's trying to X. Once we make this question explicit, however, it should be clear that we cannot answer it unless we know how, or in virtue of what, one is determined not to X, or, at least, unless we know more generally what *kind* of determinism is involved. Being determined not to X implies that something prevents one from X-ing only if one is determined *by* something that blocks the exercise of one's relevant capacities and skills. But not every kind of determinism operates this way, and it is doubtful in particular that physiological determinism does.

The characterization of ability just offered and the explanation of why, in light of it, determinism *per se* poses no threat to attributions of unexercised abilities is extremely abstract. But it was inspired by reflection on detailed and concrete, albeit imaginary, stories. In presenting one such story, I hope to bring to life the perspective on ability that I am advocating, and to make it not only more concrete and easier to grasp but also overwhelmingly plausible.

Before beginning the story, I should mention that in its significant features it is not at all original. Indeed, its value should be entirely credited to Gottfried Wilhelm Leibniz, from whose work all my thoughts on the subject of this chapter are derived. Because historical interpretation is not my concern here, however, and because some deviations from the original story make for an easier presentation, it seems best to leave Leibniz's exact views and their relation to the rest of his philosophy as far out of the discussion as possible. Our concern here is not whether anyone else ever suggested, much less believed this story. It is, for our purposes, just a story.

The Story

Once upon a time—before time, really—there was a God, who conceived of every possible world, and who decided to create the best one. Of first importance to the God of our story was that the world He created contain a certain kind of agent. In particular, the world was to contain agents who were capable not only of theoretical but of practical reason, who were therefore capable of deliberating about their actions and of choosing what to do on the basis of these deliberations. If it weren't question-begging, I would add that it was important to God that these agents be free. But, since that would be question-begging, I will say only that it was important to God that these agents *not be psychologically determined* to make the particular choices or perform the particular actions they do. That is, it was important to God that often, when these agents chose what to do, it would have been equally compatible with their psychological histories in conjunction with all the psychological laws applying to them that they had chosen something else.

In light of the tremendous significance God placed on the existence of this sort of agent, a category I shall hereafter refer to as the category of persons, God's choice to create the best of all possible worlds may now be seen as having been restricted by Him to a choice among all the possible worlds containing persons. But the persons in some worlds are better—morally better, for instance, or more amusing—than the persons in others, and the persons in some worlds do better things than the persons in other possible worlds do. The God in our story chose to create the world in which the best set of people do the best set of things.

Descending to the level of trivial detail, let us imagine that the world with the best set of people doing the best set of things contains in it a professor named Rose who, one evening after her children are in bed, turns on the television to watch *The Philadelphia Story* for the seventh time. We may imagine that there is a possible world exactly similar to the world just mentioned with respect to every event prior to the moment at which Rose turns on the TV, but in which the corresponding woman (also named Rose) decides to grade the papers from her introductory ethics course instead. Perhaps it is because, had the papers been graded, they would have been handed back the next day, and the premed student, who had written a bad paper, would have been so flustered and disappointed by his grade that he would have flunked his physics test that afternoon, that God preferred to create the first world rather than the second. In any event, God did create the first world, the world in which Rose turns on the TV. Our question is, "*Could* she have graded her papers instead?"

Let us be perfectly clear that, in choosing to create one possible world rather than another, God preordains every event that actually occurs. For, when we imagine a world in which anything happens that is different from what actually happens, we imagine a different possible world, one that, by hypothesis, God does not choose to create. God chooses to create one completely specific possible world rather than any other, and, because He is omnipotent, His choice to create that world *guarantees* (albeit mysteriously) that exactly that world will come about. In light of this, it seems undeniable that in one sense Rose could not have graded papers. For God chose to create the world in which Rose watched TV, and thereby guaranteed that she would watch TV. Given God's choice to create this world, it is impossible that Rose do anything else. (Indeed, if Rose had decided to do anything else, God would not have created this world and so Rose would not exist.)

But, *in the sense relevant to an assessment of Rose's freedom and responsibility*, could she have chosen otherwise? Can she fairly be held accountable for what she did?

Perhaps you will think that I have not given sufficient details to the case to allow you to answer this. After all, Rose could have been coerced or even hypnotized into watching TV; she could be literally addicted to TV, or obsessed with Cary Grant. Alternatively, she could have a pathological aversion to grading papers that she is helpless to overcome except in the face of, say, death threats from her students or the imminent prospect of losing her job. However, let us assume that no forces like these are at work. Rather, Rose is just someone who, while having a sense of responsibility about her job, is not exactly what you would call a workaholic. She takes her students and their anxieties seriously, but not so seriously as to give them automatic and unconditional precedence over considerations of her own self-interest. On the night in question, she thinks about whether to grade papers or watch the movie on TV. She reasons that if she does not grade those papers tonight, she will just have to grade them tomorrow, and that she could tape *The Philadelphia Story* and watch it the next night, anyway. On the other hand, she is not in the mood to grade papers, and the thought of watching Katharine Hepburn and Jimmy Stewart—and, yes, of course, Cary Grant—is appealing. It is compatible with her psychological history up to the time in question, in conjunction with all the psychological laws that apply to her, that she choose to watch the movie, and it is also compatible with these that she choose to grade papers. As it happens, she chooses to watch the movie.

Recalling that the world we are discussing is a divinely determined world, one might take issue with my use of the phrase "as it happens." For it was determined to happen, and so in a sense it had to happen. But my point is that the sense in which it had to happen has no bearing on Rose. God's choice to create a world in which a woman named Rose watches TV does not force, or even influence, Rose's decision to watch TV. (To the contrary, it was part of God's reason for choosing this world that it contain the sort of agent for whom such decisions are *not* forced.) Rose just does choose TV, then, and God, knowing that Rose will do this, chooses to create, or actualize, the world in which Rose exists.

It is natural at this point to ask how, if nothing forces Rose to turn on the TV, God *can* know that she will turn it on. Or, thinking about it from a different angle, one might ask how God can guarantee that the world He has created is the world in which a woman named Rose does turn on the TV and not the somewhat different possible world in which a woman named Rose grades papers. These questions are natural to ask because it is natural to think that one cannot know with certainty that something will happen unless one knows of some events or states of affairs that, in conjunction with some causal laws, *make* it happen, and it is natural to think that one cannot guarantee that something will happen unless one can bring about some events or states of affairs that, in conjunction with some causal laws, make it happen. Natural as it is to assume such conditions, however, it does not seem to me that *God's* knowledge and *God's* power are subject to them. God does not need a *way* of knowing, or a *way* of guaranteeing that Rose will decide to watch TV. He simply knows (or notices) that a certain possible world contains a woman named Rose who decides to watch TV, and He chooses to create that possible world. Omnipotence is not fully comprehensible.

Some people may not be willing to consider philosophical arguments that appeal to the incomprehensible power of God, even if the appeal is limited to the context of a story. I hope this will pose no problem for my argument, however, for I want now to further elaborate the story in a way that eliminates this element of opacity.

So far I have talked about God's choice to create a world with persons, and, indeed, a world in which the best set of persons do the best set of things. And I have talked, for the sake of simplicity, as if that description sufficed to identify a uniquely best world. But in fact it does not. For at least some worlds contain many objects and events that are wholly unrelated to persons and their activities, objects and events that, from God's point of view, may also be evaluatively assessed. Moreover, persons themselves may be composed of one type of stuff in one world, composed of a different type of stuff in another. And the stuff of which persons (and other things) are composed may operate according to one set of laws in one world, according to a different set of laws in another. To get quickly to the point, worlds that are exactly equivalent with respect to the value of their respective sets of persons may nonetheless differ with respect to their physics in ways that, from God's point of view, are evaluatively significant. In fact, so far as I can tell, worlds may be not just evaluatively equivalent but even exactly similar at what may be called the psychological level of description while still differing at the level of physics. In other words, there may be many worlds each of which contains a woman named Rose who watches TV on a given evening (and each of which contains all sorts of other people, each doing exactly similar things in each world) but which contain different physical laws of nature.

We have already seen that in thinking about God's choice to create the best of all possible worlds, we may think of God as restricting Himself to choosing among worlds that contain persons, and indeed, to choosing among worlds that contain maximally valuable sets of persons-and-their-actions. To narrow things down still further, we may imagine God to consider the different physical realizations of the persons in these different worlds and the different physical laws to which the stuff of which persons are composed is subject. He chooses what, for reasons that we need not fill in, He regards as the best of these. In particular, He chooses a world in which persons are composed of stuff that is subject to completely deterministic physical laws.

Those who earlier were troubled by the incomprehensibility of God's knowledge and power may now be at ease. For although I do not think we needed an answer to the question "How could God be so sure that Rose would watch the movie?" in the actual world of our elaborated story an answer is anyway available. For the world now turns out to be a physically determined world, and Rose to be composed of physical stuff. Since God created a world with initial conditions and physical laws that jointly imply that at a certain time physical movements would take place in a certain organism that would constitute the raising of an arm, the grasping and clockwise turning of a knob, the pressing of a certain button, God could be sure that Rose would watch the movie.

Descriptively speaking, our story is now complete. But we must stay within it a little while longer, long enough, in particular, to settle whether Rose, who actually watched the movie, could have graded papers instead.

It should be perfectly clear to everyone now that there is at least one sense in which she could not. For not only was it preordained by God that there should be a woman named Rose who watched a movie that night, it was physically determined that this event should come about. It was not only, so to speak, divinely impossible that

Rose should choose to grade papers, it was physically impossible as well. But our interest is in whether, in a sense relevant to an assessment of Rose's freedom and responsibility, Rose could have chosen to grade papers. Was it, in a relevant sense, up to Rose?

Let us begin by recalling what was said at an earlier point: that Rose is not coerced or hypnotized; that no addiction, obsession, or pathological aversion is involved. Rather, Rose just thinks about whether to watch TV or grade papers. It is compatible with her psychological history up to the moment in question, in conjunction with all the psychological and psychophysical laws that apply to her, that she choose TV, and it is also compatible with these that she choose to grade papers. As it happens, on the evening in question she chooses TV.

In light of the fact that Rose's choice is both divinely *and* physically determined, the outcry against the use of "as it happens" is apt to be even louder than before. Again, it was determined to happen and so it had to happen. Again, however, we need to attend to what bearing this fact has on Rose. Earlier, before the issue of physical determinism came up, I urged that God's choice to create the world in which Rose chooses to watch TV does not force or even influence Rose's choice. Nonetheless, Rose does choose TV, and God, knowing that this is what Rose does, chooses to create the world in which Rose exists. Now that we have established that this world is physically determined, it may be thought that God does force Rose after all, or that if God does not force her, physics does. God does, after all, create initial conditions and laws of nature that together imply that the organism that is Rose makes movements which are the turning on of the TV—and where the organism goes, so must Rose.

In reply to this, I must first point out that this objection only repeats what was acknowledged already—that, since it is both divinely and physically impossible that Rose grade papers, there is at least one sense in which Rose cannot grade them. Since the question I wish to raise is whether *that* sense (or those senses) is (are) relevant to assessments of freedom and responsibility, it will not help to repeat that in that sense Rose cannot do other than what she actually does. Still, the intuition that it is relevant is very strong, and some might think that no further argument is needed.

The following consideration suggests, however, that further argument *is* needed. The intuition that Rose is forced to turn on the TV, or, at least, that she has to turn on the TV, rests, it would seem, on the knowledge that Rose's body is determined to make certain movements, coupled with the thought I expressed above as "where the organism goes, so must Rose." But without further argument, there is no reason to give priority to this thought over the converse, "where Rose goes, so must the organism." Of course, in a sense both claims are equally (and completely) true, but the suggestion behind the first, which is fueling the intuition with which we are concerned, is—to put it very informally—that Rose's body controls Rose, whereas the suggestion behind the second is—again, very informally—that Rose controls her body. Somewhat less informally, and also less misleadingly, the difference between the first thought and the second may be expressed in terms of whether, in this case, the physical level of explanation of Rose's behavior is more or less basic than the psychological level of explanation of Rose's behavior.

Discussions of the relation between the psychological and the physical, of the notion of different levels of explanation, and of the idea of one level of explanation being more basic than another lead into difficult and often technical issues in the philosophy of mind and the philosophy of science into which I cannot enter here. Though the very ideas of different levels of explanation and, more specifically, of a psychological level that is neither in principle reducible to nor eliminable by physical explanations are matters of controversy, these ideas have many able proponents working to clarify and defend them against objections. Insofar as the story just presented and the following discussion appear intelligible and even plausible, this provides a reason for expecting that ultimately these ideas will be successfully defended. In the meantime, I can provide no definitions of psychological and physical levels of explanation and no analysis of what it is for one level of explanation to be more basic than another and must hope that an intuitive grasp of these concepts will suffice for the purposes for which I use them.

In order to avoid one source of confusion, however, I must stress that when I speak of a psychological *level* of explanation I do not mean to refer to a class of explanations that exclusively appeal to psychological properties and states. A bleeding ulcer, a double vodka, the presence of a very physical gun at one's back will significantly affect one's capacities for choice and action. Insofar as physical events, states, and properties interact with psychological ones, they must be available for reference at the psychological level of explanation. When I speak of a psychological level of explanation, then, I refer not to a class of exclusively psychological explanations but to a level of explanation in which psychological concepts have a significant place. Similarly, when I speak of someone as being "psychologically free" I refer to someone who is free at the level of psychological explanation, and by "psychological laws" I mean laws at the level of psychological explanation.

As I have pointed out, the intuition that its being physically impossible for Rose to do anything but turn on the TV renders Rose unable, in the relevant sense, to grade papers presupposes that, in this case, the physical level of explanation is more basic than the psychological level. But a recollection of the way our story began suggests quite the opposite position, viz., that in this case—indeed, in this world—the psychological level is more basic than the physical. For recall that in God's choosing which world to create it was of the *first* importance to God that the world contain agents to whom a certain kind of explanation applied—agents who could act according to their choices, who could choose according to their deliberations, and for whom it was not psychologically determined what choices they would make and what actions they would perform. This being established, it was of next importance that it be a world with a maximally valuable set of agents doing a maximally valuable set of things. The choices among different possible sets of physical laws, much less different possible physical initial conditions, were, then, of tertiary or lower levels of importance. It is as if God first chose what set of people-and-their-actions to create and then chose how best to physically realize that set.

Returning one last time to Rose as she contemplates what to do that evening, recall that, at the psychological level of explanation, she *can* choose TV or paper-grading. Does the fact that, at the physical level of explanation, it is determined that she will choose TV imply that, in a relevant sense, she cannot choose paper-grading after all? This depends on the answer to the following question: Do the physical facts make Rose choose (or explain why she chooses) to watch TV, or does Rose's choice to watch TV make (or explain why) the physical facts come out as they do? Given God's basis for choosing which world to create, the latter seems more reasonable than the former. For God's choice of the physical facts does not condition but rather is conditioned *by* His choice of the psychological or personal facts. God wanted (among other things) to create a world in which a woman named Rose watches TV one evening while being psychologically able at that time to grade papers instead, and He chose a set of physical laws and initial conditions that have (among other things) the property of harmonizing with this state of affairs. In light of this, it seems wrong to think of the physical facts, determined though they are, as making Rose watch TV. They merely constitute the physical realization of her psychologically free choice.

Rose's situation when deciding how to spend her evening, then, includes the following two salient features: First, Rose has all the skills, talents, and capacities that are necessary for her to grade papers. She has the requisite knowledge, judgment, and experience to evaluate the students' work as fairly and intelligently as the average philosophy teacher. Second, nothing interferes with or prevents her from exercising these skills, talents, and capacities. There is ink in her pen, a light at her desk, she is not prohibitively tired or sick, she has no pathological aversion to paper-grading or anything of that sort.

It might be thought that the fact that Rose is physically determined to choose to watch TV implies that *something* must prevent her from exercising the skills, talents, and capacities necessary for grading papers. But I do not see why this should be so. Particularly when one reflects on the fact that God chose to create a world with the relevant physical facts only after choosing to create a world with the relevant psychological facts—that, in other words, He chose to create that particular set of physical laws of nature in conjunction with that particular set of initial conditions only after, and partly in order to harmonize with, His choice to create a woman named Rose who would make a psychologically free choice for TV—it is hard to see the physical facts as constraining Rose's choice.

If one holds firmly to the belief that the psychological level of explanation is as basic as or more basic than any other level of explanation with respect to Rose's action, then, the ability to do otherwise relevant to an assessment of Rose's freedom and responsibility seems to be discernible at the psychological level of explanation alone. If Rose is psychologically free to grade papers—if, in particular, it is compatible with Rose's psychological history and all the psychological and psychophysical laws that apply to her that she does grade papers—then it seems to me that she *can* (is able to) grade papers in any sense that might be relevant to an assessment of her freedom and responsibility.

The Moral of the Story

Justifications must come to an end somewhere, and mine comes to an end here, with an appeal to your intuitions about the case I have described. My hope is that, once you separate the question of Rose's *psychological* ability to do otherwise from issues about the physical possibility or impossibility of her doing so, you will think, as I do, that the psychological ability to do otherwise is all the ability it makes sense for someone to care about. One last point of clarification about what psychological ability is, however, may allay some persisting doubts.

In particular, it may be helpful explicitly to distinguish psychological ability from what may be called epistemological ability. Let us say that a person has the epistemological ability to X if and only if, for all anyone (including the agent herself) knows, she can X. The view that the epistemological ability to do otherwise is all that is relevant to issues of freedom and responsibility has, I believe, been suggested by others, but it does not seem plausible to me. The following example will show why.

Tony, the son of a Mafia don, has reached a turning point in his life. He must decide whether to follow in his father's footsteps as a leader in organized crime, or instead to break completely from his family to lead a life as an honest schoolteacher. He believes that it is in his power to choose either path, that he is aware of the costs and benefits on each side, that he can assess them rationally and act on whatever, as a result of his tortured deliberations, he decides. Reasoning that if he doesn't take over his father's position his more ruthless and less intelligent brother will, and that his leaving the family would break his mother's heart, he decides to remain. Tony, and presumably everyone else, believes that Tony could have chosen otherwise. But this is an illusion. In fact, Tony's fear of his father's wrath—a consequence of his possible decision to become a schoolteacher to which Tony consciously accorded some, but limited weight—was greater than Tony, or anyone else, knew, and had the unconscious effect of shaping his deliberative processes, making him attach inordinate weight to certain factors and inordinately little to others so as to produce a rationalized decision that his uncontrollable unconscious fears compelled him to reach.

Since, for all Tony knew, he was able to choose otherwise, we may imagine that Tony regarded himself as fully responsible for his decision. Nonetheless, it seems to me that Tony was not fully responsible, and this because he wasn't *really* able to choose anything else, in a sense that is relevant to assessments of freedom and responsibility. Note, however, that this sense is a sense that is captured at the psychological level of explanation. For, despite what Tony and everyone else thinks, it is not really compatible with Tony's psychological history and all the psychological laws that apply to him that he choose to break with his family. Despite what Tony and everyone else thinks, there is something—namely, fear of his father's wrath—that prevents Tony from exercising his capacities in that direction. Although Tony is, if you like, epistemologically free to choose otherwise, he is not psychologically free to choose otherwise, and therefore he is not fully responsible.

This example will, I hope, bring out the fact that psychological freedom is a good deal more substantive than epistemological freedom. Epistemological freedom, we might say, is only apparent freedom. By contrast, psychological freedom is real. (Indeed, it may not be apparent—for a weak-willed person may deceive herself, thinking that she is not psychologically able to do what, as a matter of fact, she is able to do.) I believe that psychological freedom is what incompatibilist intuitions, sympathetically understood, are about. The point of the elaborate story involving God and Rose and ungraded papers was that it offered a setting in which psychological freedom could be pried apart from physical freedom without its status being thereby reduced or belittled.

Still, the world of Rose and her students is not our world, and so someone may ask, "What has all this to do with us?" It is, as I said at the outset, just a story. The story has a moral, however, or perhaps two morals, one negative and one positive. Its negative moral is that the abilities necessary for responsibility, even the unexercised abilities, are not *as such* incompatible with divine or physical determinism. Its being divinely or physically impossible that A do X does not imply that A lacks the ability to do X, that A cannot do X, in any sense relevant to the assessment of A's responsibility. It is not, then part of the *meaning* of "ability" or "can" used in contexts of responsibility-assessment that they imply physical (or divine) possibility. Though the world of Rose and her students is not our world, it is *a* world in which determinism—indeed, both divine and physical determinism—and the freedom necessary for responsibility coexist. And so, if someone wants to argue that physical determinism and freedom cannot coexist in our world, she must explain what it is about our world that implies that conclusion in our case. Admittedly, God's creation of the world in our story, and His reasons for creating that world rather than another, were crucial to our establishing that the physical level of explanation was not more basic—was arguably even less basic—than the psychological level. We cannot appeal to these features in discussing our world. But mere withdrawal of these features is not sufficient to imply the reverse conclusion that in our world the physical level of explanation is more basic than the psychological. Without that conclusion there seems no reason to think that explanations of our actions at the physical level are any more relevant to assessments of our freedom and responsibility than they are to an assessment of Rose's.[2]

The negative moral of the story, then, is that arguments or appeals to intuition that move directly from "It is determined that A do X" or "It is impossible that A do X" to "A cannot do other than X, in a sense relevant to freedom and responsibility" are inadequate. A convincing argument for incompatibilism must go deeper than that. A more positive lesson can be learned from the story, however, if we ask ourselves what it is about Rose and the other persons in her world that leads us to conclude that they are able to do otherwise in the sense relevant to freedom and responsibility, and why it is that divine and physical determinism pose no threat to them.

The answer to the first question lies, I believe, in the fact that although Rose and her fellow persons are divinely and physically determined, they are not psychologically determined—that is, they are not determined at the psychological level of explanation.[3] In light of this, occasions arise in which they are faced with choices for which they have all the skills, talents, and capacities necessary for choosing one way *or* the other, and in which nothing prevents them from exercising their skills, talents, and so on to either end. Recalling the disjunctive characterization of ability offered earlier in this chapter, this means that the kinds of determinism that apply to their world are not such as to deprive them of the sorts of ability relevant to assessments of responsibility.

The answer to the second question lies, I believe, in the fact that Rose's world is one in which a very natural assumption is seen to be unwarranted—namely, the assumption that if it is divinely or physically determined that one do X, then it must be the case that something prevents one from doing anything other than X, or perhaps that something interferes with one's ability not to do X. This assumption is unwarranted in the case of Rose and her fellow persons. God does not interfere with Rose. He just decides to create her, knowing in advance what she will freely choose to do. Similarly, physics does not interfere with her—it just goes ineluctably on, providing, in unconscious harmony, a physical realization of Rose's choices.

The tendency to think that physical determinism must interfere with our psychological freedom comes, I believe, from the thought, "Given physical conditions and laws just as they are, my behavior is determined *regardless* of what I want, think, and choose."[4] When we keep the physical facts fixed, in other words, our psychologies seem irrelevant. One of the points of this chapter was to raise doubts about the status of this act of imagination. Why should we keep the physical facts fixed, while imagining our psychologies to go haywire? Why not instead keep the psychological facts fixed and vary the physical ones? The latter is no more and no less serious a "possibility," than the former, but when we focus on it, the threat of physical determinism goes away.

In the absence of further argument, there seems no reason to take physical facts and explanations more seriously than psychological ones, even in cases where physical explanations are deterministic and psychological ones are not. In the absence of further argument, then, there seems no reason to think that the truth of divine or physical determinism would imply that everyone lacks the abilities to choose and to act in accordance with Reason that are needed in order to be a responsible being.

It is worth pointing out that if, nonetheless, there turn out to be reasons to take physical facts and explanations more seriously than psychological ones, if the physical level of explanation turns out to be more basic, more deep, more real than the psychological one, this would call into question a good deal more than an agent's ability to act according to Reason (especially at a time when she in fact fails to do so). It would call into question the status of the very language of ability, choice, and human agency. It would call into question not only the possibility of a *free* will, but the very meaningfulness of describing events in terms of wills, or even persons, at all.

Meanwhile, we may, perhaps we must, continue to operate within a framework according to which beings like ourselves are understood to be persons capable of intentional action. Only within this framework does the question of whether we are or can be responsible beings make sense.

6

The True and the Good

(In Which the Metaethical Assumptions
of the Reason View Are Examined)

According to the Reason View, a person's status as a responsible agent rests not only on her ability to make her behavior conform to her deepest values but also on her ability to form, assess, and revise those values on the basis of a recognition and appreciation of what I have called the True and the Good. In other words, in addition to the requirement that the agent be able to govern her behavior by her reasons, the Reason View holds that an agent must be in a position that allows her reasons to be governed by what reasons there are.

This second condition is perhaps the most distinctive and controversial feature of the Reason View. The fundamental idea behind it is that an agent cannot have the kind of freedom and control necessary for responsibility unless, when making choices about values and actions, she can understand the significant features of her situation and of the alternatives among which her choice is to be made. That is, an agent cannot be free and responsible unless she can sufficiently see and appreciate the world (or the relevant portion of it) for what it is.

Most important, the idea of "seeing and appreciating the world for what it is" must be understood to comprehend not only having an accurate and sufficiently wide set of empirical beliefs but also having a correct and sufficiently broad appreciation of normative issues. Seeing the world correctly, as I understand it, involves seeing not only what is true and false but also what is valuable and worthless. That is why, in describing what is required for responsibility, I have spoken of the ability to act in accordance with the True *and the Good*. But, of course, the meaning of this abstract phrase is far from clear, and, given the phrase's dangerously Platonic overtones, the apparent commitment to the objectivity of value is nothing if not controversial. I have suggested that responsibility involves the ability to act in accordance with the True and the Good. But if one is uncertain that there *is* a True and a Good, one may dismiss my analysis as nonsense. Indeed, even those who are firmly convinced of the existence of objective values may reasonably be suspicious of an account of free and responsible agency that depends on this conviction.

In this chapter, I take up the question of what degree and what type of objectivity of value my analysis of responsibility presupposes. I shall argue that the necessary metaethical assumptions about objectivity are in fact quite weak and extremely plausible, and that even those who are not convinced of these assumptions should not be surprised to find a conceptual link between them and the concept of responsibility.

Because the metaethical assumptions presupposed by the Reason View are quite weak, a great variety of metaethical positions are compatible with it. Still, some of these views are more plausible than others, and the one that seems to me the most plausible seems especially to complement and be complemented by the conception of freedom and responsibility that the Reason View embodies. This chapter ends with the presentation of that view, which I call Normative Pluralism, and of the vision of the free and responsible agent that emerges when the Reason View is placed in the context of that view.

The Role of "the True and the Good" in the Reason View

In order to see what kind of objectivity is presupposed by the Reason View, we need to be able to sketch and understand the range of possible positions people may hold on this subject. This is difficult, because the language in which this issue is discussed is (perhaps unavoidably) slippery. Statements that are intended to capture and express one view continually seem open to interpretations that are in the opposite spirit. Thus, for example, disagreements about whether value judgments can be true or false are typically understood in such a way as to associate a positive answer to this question with an objectivist conception of value. However, a proponent of the view that evaluative judgments are analyzable as judgments about what society approves or disapproves of will accept the positive claim in a spirit that is antithetical to objectivism. Similarly, the claim that one can (or cannot) derive an "ought" from an "is," or that ethics is (or is not) very different from science, can, in context, form part of a view that is substantially opposed to the one these remarks initially suggest.

In the next section, I shall offer my own description of the metaethical spectrum and point out how large a portion of it is compatible with the conception of responsibility that I have proposed. Before I do so, however, it will be useful to recall the role that "the True and the Good" and other phrases that equally suggest a commitment to objective values play in the development of the Reason View. Keeping that role in mind and interpreting these phrases in their relevant context make it reasonable from the outset to expect that only very weak metaethical presumptions underlie these phrases and that, in particular, no metaethical presumptions are made that are not already part of moral common sense.

In earlier chapters I have drawn attention to the tendency to regard external features of the world that shape, govern, or determine an agent's behavior as inimical to an agent's freedom and responsibility. While this attitude seems obviously appropriate in regard to features that control an agent independently of her own beliefs and values, reflection encourages us to apply this attitude more broadly, toward features of the world that control the agent's beliefs and values themselves. As Chapters 3 and 4 have argued, however, generalizations of this attitude are insupportable if applied to *all* external features that can affect an agent's beliefs. Since human agents live within a world of facts already established, knowledge *of* the world, and therefore knowledge necessarily shaped *by* the world, in which they must act is, for the most part, promotive of freedom and responsibility rather than inimical to it.

This is easy to see when we focus on unequivocally nonevaluative facts. One is less responsible for one's actions, not more, if one cannot know what these actions really are or be aware of their probable consequences. A man living in a fantasy world is not responsible for making a spectacle of himself railing, for example, at a German Sheperd he takes to be an incarnation of the devil. A woman whose suitcase has been switched for another is not responsible for carrying illegal drugs across the border. No one would suggest that freedom *from* empirical evidence is a valuable kind of freedom to have when forming scientific beliefs. No one wants beliefs about her immediate environment to be free *from* sensory input.

Having one's beliefs shaped by the world, then, is not all bad, and, more to the point, it is not always a qualification on or a hindrance to one's freedom and responsibility. We can illustrate this point most easily and dramatically by noting the desirability of our knowledge of physical features of the world, which obviously relies on things that are literally external to the agent. The point, however, is not about the formation of scientific or empirical beliefs exclusively, but about the formation of *any* beliefs the truth or falsehood of which is outside of the agent's control. As it is not up to me to choose whether begonia leaves are poisonous, it is not up to me to choose whether the number nineteen is prime. As no one wants one's physical beliefs to be free from empirical evidence, no one wants one's mathematical and logical beliefs to be free from the effects that intelligent reflection, good teaching, and rigorous argument are apt to have. The positive connection between freedom and responsibility and the potential influence of external features of the world that, in conjunction with sound powers of perception and reasoning, give us true beliefs may be captured by the slogan that the free and responsible agent must be able to see and appreciate the True.

But if the world in which we live contains evaluative as well as nonevaluative facts, then the reasoning that leads us to see the connection between responsibility and the ability to see the True will similarly lead us to connect responsibility with receptiveness to the Good. Indeed, strictly speaking, on this view, the Good just constitutes part of the True, for, if there are evaluative facts, they are plainly a subset of all the facts. Once one is convinced that understanding one's situation and one's options enhances one's ability to make free and responsible choices, one must admit that moral, aesthetic, and, more generally, normative understanding will enhance that ability no less significantly than understanding in other areas.

Abstract references to "receptiveness to the Good," "moral knowledge," and "evaluative facts" tend to arouse philosophical concern. More concrete illustrations of the point of these references, however, may render these phrases innocuous. Thus, let us first imagine a man who must choose which of two switches to pull. It seems obvious that, if he does not and cannot know that one of them will turn on a light while the other will send an electric shock through a young boy in the next room, the man is not morally responsible for which of these effects he brings about. But what if he does know of these effects, and he also knows that electric shocks are horribly painful, but he does not know and cannot know that there is anything *wrong* with shocking people? Admittedly, it is difficult fully to imagine a person who is incapable of recognizing such a basic moral truth as this. But when we do imagine someone who is so incapacitated, whether as a result of severe mental retardation or extreme sociopathology, we readily conclude that this mental deficiency removes him from the sphere of moral responsibility as much as does more narrowly defined (nonculpable) factual ignorance. The inability to know right from wrong is universally recognized as a sufficient condition of criminal insanity.

A second type of case concerns people who, though evidently capable of appreciating some basic moral attitudes and judgments, nonetheless exhibit gaps in their moral understanding that are most naturally explained by factors in their upbringings and their social environments more generally. Consider the ordinary citizen living in Germany in the 1930s, the white child brought up on a southern plantation in the 1850s, or anyone brought up forty years ago to become a "lady" or a "gentleman" and to accept conventional sex roles as deep features of human nature or civilized society. Although it would be difficult to establish, even in individual cases, that such people were unable to see and appreciate the injustice of some of the practices, attitudes, and institutions of their communities, insofar as we do regard social pressures and norms as potential obstacles to sound moral judgments, we lessen the blame we would otherwise direct toward individuals who, surrounded by these obstacles, fail to reach these judgments.

The determination that an individual is unable to see and appreciate important moral truths is one of considerable moral consequence, and therefore one that we should be wary of making. Criminal insanity is obviously a very grave charge. And if we too readily excuse people for accepting injustice that is embedded in their societies' ethical codes, we will encourage conformity and a kind of moral laziness that will foster the hidden injustices that remain. Nonetheless, we cannot even consider this determination, we cannot even regard it as a logical possibility, without implicitly revealing a commitment to objective values on a par with that entailed by the Reason View. We cannot wonder whether the sadist who sees nothing wrong with torture is sick or just plain evil unless we are confident that there *is* something wrong with torture, and that people whose emotional and intellectual capacities fall within a normal range are able correctly to recognize that this is so. We cannot imagine excusing a person for failing to oppose slavery without the implicit presumption that slavery deserves to be opposed, and that a more enlightened social environment allows or even forces people to see this.

The ability to recognize and appreciate the True and the Good refers to nothing more exotic than the ability to see and understand what is true and what is good, or, to put it differently, the ability to acquire true beliefs rather than false ones and good values rather than bad ones, and to understand these beliefs and values sufficiently to be able to make proper use of them. Insofar as these concepts constitute a commitment to objectivity, the naturalness of the very discussion of limited responsibility for certain sorts of wrongdoers suggests that this commitment is no greater than that embedded in ordinary moral thought.

As a defense of the claim that values are objective, the argument that it is implicit in common sense is weak at best. A belief's being common does not guarantee its being true. Given the long history and complexity of the issue it addresses, a full-scale defense of the claim that values are objective is far beyond the scope of this treatise. Nonetheless, the recognition that the commitment to objectivity implicit in such phrases as "the True and the Good" and "what reasons there are" as they are used throughout this book is no greater than the commitment implicit in much concrete and ordinary moral discourse should discourage us from reading in esoteric metaphysical and epistemological assumptions that these phrases might suggest if taken out of context. In fact, I suspect that there is a tendency to read more into these phrases than is necessary whether or not one regards them as expressions or implications of common sense, and that much of the attractiveness of subjectivism, the position that denies all objectivity to values, depends on its being seen as the only alternative to an implausibly rigid and absolutist normative view. Although I shall not attempt a full-scale defense of the thesis that values are, in the relevant sense, objective, I shall point out how much (and how little!) is implied by it. It may be that a clear understanding of the thesis will itself defuse a considerable portion of the resistance it tends to arouse.

The Metaethical Spectrum

To clear the ground, we can quickly dismiss some of the connotations that "the ability to see and appreciate the True and the Good" might have that are irrelevant and unnecessary to its use in context. The Platonic suggestion that the True and the Good are *things* that exist in some other world, or the idea that reasons and values have an ontological status akin to that of tables and chairs, obviously has no connection to the analysis of responsibility offered by the Reason View. Nor does the proposal that correct values can literally be *seen*, or apprehended by a special faculty that is similar to a form of sense perception. An objectivist account of values need be neither crudely intuitionist nor crudely Platonic. The acquisition of good values, like the acquisition of true beliefs, may require the exercise of a variety of faculties and depend on a background of some suitable range of experience.

The most plausible objectivist account of values, I think, is one that holds that perception, imagination, reflection, training, and the powers of logical thinking are all relevant to at least some instances of acceptable methods of reaching value judgments. In this respect, the acquisition of sound value judgments is no different from the acquisition of sound nonevaluative beliefs.

Finally, discussion of the True *and* the Good should not be understood to suggest that facts and values are two separate but equally objective realms. Indeed, maintaining a distinction between facts and values is apt to encourage a less plausible form of objectivism than might be developed without it, and might lead one to expect analogies between truth and goodness, or between truth-related and value-related notions, that other perspectives would show to be forced and artificial. As I have already suggested, a more plausible form of normative objectivism would regard the Good simply as part of the True, or, more precisely, it would regard the set of correct value judgments as a subset of the set of correct judgments (or propositions) period, and not necessarily a sharply delineable subset at that.

Reference to the Reason View's requirement that a responsible agent be capable of acting in accordance with the True and the Good, then, should not be taken to imply the existence of a principled distinction between the True and the Good. Rather, it is a way of calling attention to the fact that the psychological features a responsible agent are required to have must include normative as well as nonnormative competence.

What the Reason View does assume is that it makes sense to talk of "normative competence" and to ask whether a given individual possesses it. This in turn implies the existence of nonarbitrary standards of correctness, standards that are independent of an individual's will and even of an individual's psychology as a whole, by which one can judge some actions, choices, ways of life, or systems of value to be better than others. To this extent, the Reason View does implicitly contain a commitment to the objectivity of value. But this commitment falls far short of what people often understand an objective position on values to entail.

In particular, although this position embraces the existence of nonarbitrary standards of correctness for value judgments, it need not assume that these standards determine a unique, universally applicable, complete, and optimal system of values and value judgments, nor need it assume the availability or even the intelligibility of a culture-independent point of view from which these standards are understood to have been generated. What is relevant to responsibility, according to the Reason View, is that the agent be capable of forming better values rather than worse ones, good value judgments rather than bad ones, just insofar as there *are* better and worse choices and judgments to be made. According to the Reason View, the responsible agent must be in a position that allows the reasons she has for a choice to be governed by the reasons there are. But if the reasons there are fail to determine a uniquely right or best choice, the agent is no less responsible an agent for that.

Of course, if there were a single and complete best set of values and value judgments that, if we could but see the world rightly, we all would share, then the Reason View would imply that the maximally free and responsible agent be capable of discovering and understanding that set. But if values are only partly constrained by Reason, broadly construed, then, according to the Reason View, an agent can be free and responsible so long as she is able to form, consider, and revise her values and value judgments in ways that are sufficiently guided by these constraints.

In light of this, it should be clear that the Reason View is compatible with many forms of relativism. For the view that, even at a basic level, what values are correct for a person is in part a function of the conventions, institutions, expectations, and attitudes of that person's community need not deny that alongside or even within this context there are nonconventional and nonarbitrary standards for assessing some values, actions, and judgments as better than others.

The Reason View is also compatible with a position that may seem even more normatively tolerant than that. For one may hold that although Reason constrains values, it does not constrain them completely, even when the conventions and shared understandings of a person's community and the concrete details of her more specific situation are taken into account. One may believe that there are good grounds for judging some values to be better than others without believing that appeal to such grounds will yield a complete ordering of principles and values that contains a determinate answer to every well-formed question. One may believe that child abuse is unequivocally wrong (or even, more weakly, that a particular instance of it is) without being committed to the position that there is a fact of the matter about the morality of positive euthanasia. This view, which I call Normative Pluralism, is perhaps most naturally described as one according to which values and value judgments are *partially* objective. It will be discussed at greater length at the end of the chapter. For now, what is important to recognize is that such a view, insofar as it distinguishes evaluative positions that are within Reasonable bounds from those which are not, has a place for the notion of normative competence. It is therefore objective *enough* to be available to a proponent of the Reason View.

The only position not available to a proponent of the Reason View, then, would seem to be one that denies the objectivity of values completely and insists that there are no nonarbitrary standards independent of the individual agent on the basis of which some values or systems of value can be defended as preferable to others. The antiobjectivist position just stated, however, is ambiguous—indeed, doubly ambiguous—in a way that makes even its implications for the Reason View unclear.

Varieties of Antiobjectivism

People often begin to doubt the objectivity of values upon trying to justify their own values and finding their attempts unsatisfactory. (Analogies to the paths that lead to other forms of skepticism are easy to make.) Thus, we can see how a person who formerly assumed that morality derived from a God whose existence she has begun to doubt, or a person who is suddenly struck by the logical weakness of standard forms of moral argument, or a person who, being introduced to the sharply contrasting moral attitudes of another culture, cannot find any intercultural basis for preferring one culture's code to the other, might come to wonder whether all her values are, in fact, unsupported. Such reflections, however, may lead people to one of at least three possible antiobjectivist positions, only one of which is, so far as I can tell, strictly incompatible with the Reason View.

Thus, one position that may arise out of such reflections revolves centrally around the claim that there is no ideal, God's-eye point of view, independent of culturally, biologically, and socially induced norms, from which systems of value can be objectively assessed. The antiobjectivist's main point, on this interpretation, is that one cannot intelligibly step completely outside of one's values when evaluating values, whether one's own or another's. What is here said about values, however, may be said with equal plausibility about nonevaluative facts. The notion of a God's-eye point of view is apt to be as intelligible or unintelligible in one context as in another.

Although there are evident grounds for calling the global position just sketched a form of antiobjectivism, its specific implications for the interpretation of value judgments might just as well be thought to constitute an anthropocentric form of objectivism. For such a position need not deny that value judgments may be true or false, or that some values are *really* better, or more rational, than others, as long as care is taken to avoid an analysis of "true" or "rational" or "really better" in terms of a standard independent of human beings. Whatever way the global antiobjectivist has of making sense of better and worse nonevaluative claims can presumably also be used to make sense of better and worse evaluative claims. Thus, the global antiobjectivist should have no trouble with the idea that we should want to be able to understand the significant normative and nonnormative features of our situations, or with the suggestion that we can be in control of our lives and responsible for our behavior only if we are able to choose and to act in light of a sufficiently full normative and nonnormative understanding.

More often, however, reasons for withdrawing claims of objectivity to values are not recognized as supporting similar withdrawals of nonevaluative claims. To the contrary, it is supposed that the thinking that undermines one's belief in the objectivity of values also points to a deep and systematic difference between values and facts. But what difference? Here again it seems that two different positions need to be distinguished, only one of which is problematic for a defender of the Reason View.

The first and most natural way to understand the denial of objectivity specifically with respect to values is as an expression of the substantive normative position of nihilism. According to this position, although Reason (broadly construed) clearly supports belief in some nonevaluative statements over others, it is indifferent among all possible values and sets of values. Though Reason urges us to believe that snow is white and not green, that three is odd and not even, that the earth revolves around the sun and not vice versa, it gives us no basis for preferring peace to war, kindness to cruelty, or pleasure to pain. Thus, the position that torture or rape is wrong is no more justified by Reason than its opposite. Since no values are justified by Reason, equally, none are condemned. This position, though morally appalling, is frequently, if often temporarily, espoused.

For some purposes, philosophers distinguish between nihilism, a position that holds that there are no objective values, and moral skepticism, which allows the possible existence of objective values but claims that, at any rate, humans cannot ever know about such values. Since both views share the common claim that no values or value judgments are supported by Reason, they may be treated as equivalent for the purpose of understanding their relation to the Reason View of responsibility.

The path to nihilism, however, may also lead one further, to a philosophical position that I shall call Conceptual Subjectivism, or subjectivism for short. According to this position, the conventional view that some values are more supportable by Reason than others is mistaken, not because, as a matter of fact, Reason is indifferent among values, but because the idea of applying Reason, understood as a nonarbitrary standard of judgment independent of an individual agent, to the assignment of values is conceptually confused.

We may bring out the contrast between nihilism and subjectivism by appeal to a distinction between "values" and "value judgments." If we use the terms "value" and "disvalue" to refer respectively to certain kinds of positive and negative attitudes, we may use the term "value judgment" to refer to the assignment of these attitudes to activities, qualities, and things. If one values humility, one will judge it to be good; if one disvalues poverty, one will judge it to be bad. But the judgment that something is neither good nor bad, but, as it were, evaluatively neutral, will also naturally be understood as a value judgment; it assigns the object a place on an evaluative continuum.

The nihilist, convinced that Reason offers no support for one value rather than another, concludes that, from the point of view of Reason, all acts and qualities are neutral. Since there is no rational justification for objecting to killing, the nihilist concludes that killing is *not* wrong. Since there is no rational justification for advocating honesty, honesty is no more than *all* right.

From a subjectivist perspective, however, the nihilist draws her conclusions too soon. If Reason doesn't support a positive attitude to some things and a negative attitude to others, neither does it support an attitude of indifference or neutrality to all things. According to the subjectivist, Reason is silent, not neutral, on questions of value. Not only does it fail to support one value over another; it fails to support one value judgment over another, including the judgment that anything goes. Thus, where the nihilist would say that "killing is bad" is no better justified than "killing is good," the subjectivist would add that "killing is neither bad nor good" is no better justified than the other alternatives.

Where the nihilist questions the content of ordinary moral thought, the subjectivist, both more and less radical, questions its categories. According to the subjectivist, it is a conceptual mistake to think Reason could *possibly* have anything to say, at least about basic values. This allows the subjectivist to keep all the value judgments the nihilist gives up. Rather than changing her substantive moral position, the subjectivist reinterprets it.

We may highlight the differences between nihilism and subjectivism and note their different implications for the Reason View by contrasting the positions they respectively entail regarding the notion of normative competence. The idea of normative competence is the idea that just as there is a set of psychological dispositions and capacities the possession of which tends to allow someone to recognize and appreciate the True, so there is a set of psychological dispositions and capacities the possession of which tends to allow someone to recognize and appreciate the Good. Whereas the nihilist would argue that since there is no Good, there is nothing to be recognized and appreciated, the subjectivist would claim that while there may be a Good, it is not the sort of thing that *can* be recognized and appreciated.

In a way, the nihilist does not dispute the notion of normative competence—she just believes that, when the normatively competent person applies herself to the search for correct values, she comes up empty. She finds that, in fact, Reason is indifferent among values. By contrast, the subjectivist does not regard her position as a rational basis for any substantive change in values. She disputes not the conclusions of ordinary moral thought but their interpretation *as* conclusions of patterns of thought that have any claim to being better, more rational, more insightful, more promotive of *correct* judgments than any others. From her point of view, the very notion of normative competence is misguided, resting as it does on the assumption that value judgments are like (or a subset of) factual judgments in being subject to authoritative assessment on the basis of standards external to the agent's psychology.

Despite the significant theoretical differences between nihilism and subjectivism, however, it is very difficult to keep these two positions apart. This is because even extreme differences in the value judgments of the proponents of these positions need not show up in practice. Although the nihilist has given up the value judgments we may assume she formerly made (that rape and torture are wrong, for example, and that kindness and justice are good), she need not have given up her preferences for the things she formerly valued or have ceased to engage in activities that will promote their realization. Her former values are demoted or reduced to the status of mere preferences, but they may remain intense preferences nonetheless. Though the nihilist is convinced that nothing justifies her negative attitude to murder, for example, she may continue to hate murder and to want to see all murderers in jail. Her nihilism commits her to the position that, objectively, the murderer has no reason not to murder. To punish him for murdering, then, and, as significantly, to threaten prospective murderers with punishment, is just to bully them into behaving as she (along with others) wants them to behave. Still, she may reply that there is no reason (that is, no objective reason) *not* to bully people into doing what one wants.

At this point, nihilism may seem virtually to transform itself into subjectivism. At any rate, the difference between these positions may seem largely verbal. These verbal differences, however, focusing as they do on the proper way to describe the activity of engaging in moral discourse, reflect differences in attitude and feeling that are of central importance in attributions of responsibility. Consequently, these differences reflect corresponding differences in the implications these positions have for the adequacy of the Reason View.

Curiously, the substantive position of nihilism, though deeply contrary in spirit to the thoughts out of which the Reason View emerged, is not strictly incompatible with it. Rather, for the nihilist, the ability to recognize the True and the Good simply collapses into the ability to recognize the True. More precisely, the ability to recognize whatever significant features of the agent's situation and options there are to be recognized invokes a category that, for the nihilist, consists wholly of nonnormative facts. The idea of choosing in accordance with true beliefs and good values, then, collapses into that of choosing in light of the facts—in light, for example, of the fact that making this movement will turn on the light or that the powder one is considering putting into the coffee is poison.

It is worth pointing out that, to the nihilist, the claim that there are no normative facts will itself seem a nonnormative fact,[1] and the ability to recognize and appreciate this may well be significant to assessing an agent's responsibility for her actions. Such a position is in fact suggested by the stress on authenticity or good faith so common in the writings of declared nihilists.

What tension there is between the Reason View and nihilism, then, lies not in the Reason View's conception of responsibility but in the judgments of blameworthiness and praiseworthiness that, from more common moral standpoints, this conception of responsibility would support. For although, as I have said, a certain kind of nihilist may consistently maintain the overt practices of punishment and reward, she can no longer regard these practices as expressions of deep praise and blame. Not believing that there is anything really right or good about what she likes or that there is anything wrong or bad about that to which she is averse, she cannot believe that anyone deserves praise or blame, credit or discredit, for conforming or failing to conform to her preferences. In light of this, the concept of responsibility that it is the aim of the Reason View to illuminate is likely to lose its interest for us, except as a means of marking off those actions which can most properly be regarded as examples of a Romantic sort of self-expression.

The subjectivist is in a different position. Where the nihilist sees her values as reduced to nonrational preferences, the subjectivist agrees that values *are* nonrational preferences but does not see them as "reduced" for all that. Although she agrees with the nihilist that her values cannot be objectively justified, the fault lies not in the values but in the inappropriate expectations, engendered no doubt by a history of philosophical confusion, about what values should (and can) be. Thus, while the nihilist believes that the cold-blooded murderer has not done anything that is objectively wrong, and therefore does not deserve blame for her action even if she is fully responsible for it, the subjectivist may believe that cold-blooded murder *is* wrong (as wrong, that is, as it is conceptually possible for anything to be) and that therefore if the murderer is responsible for her action she does deserve blame for it (that is, in whatever sense it is conceptually possible for anyone to deserve blame for anything).

I must confess that subjectivism is so alien to me and so difficult for me to sympathize with that I fear I do not fully or properly understand it. Nonetheless, since the position holds an important place in philosophical ethics and since it has been and continues to be held by philosophers of great distinction, I wish to consider it, and its implications for the Reason View, in the most powerful form I can.

If subjectivism is correct, then the notion of normative competence on which the Reason View relies ultimately makes no sense. In that case, the Reason View cannot be thought to offer a coherent account of responsibility: Either the concept of responsibility itself is incoherent or the Reason View's account of it is wrong. Believing that responsibility is a coherent concept and that the Reason View provides a correct account of it, then, commits one to believing that subjectivism is false.

Conceptual Subjectivism's Implications for the Reason View

Although I do believe that subjectivism is false, and shall offer some remarks to support this, a full-scale refutation of this position, were it possible at all, is not necessary to defend the current enterprise. For even if subjectivism were correct, this would not necessarily call into question the analysis of responsibility that the Reason View proposes. Rather, the confusions inherent in the notions invoked by the Reason View may reflect an incoherence in the concept of responsibility itself.

In light of the degree to which objectivity of values, in the weak sense that the Reason View presupposes, is embedded in common sense, the conclusion that the concept of responsibility has inherited this commitment should not seem surprising. And, indeed, insofar as I am able to take up the perspective of subjectivism, this conclusion seems internally appealing as well. That is, from the point of view of the subjectivist, the concept of responsibility does *not* seem wholly intelligible.

How, for example, is a subjectivist to make sense of the fact that young children are regarded as less responsible than older ones, that, say, a seven-year-old will be regarded as less blameworthy than a seventeen-year-old for unkind behavior? In cases of fatigue or illness, perhaps, it is reasonable to suppose that the younger child has less control of her behavior. But in other cases, at least part of the explanation for holding the younger child less responsible is that she doesn't know any better, or, more precisely, that she doesn't know *as well* as the teenager that cruelty is wrong. Being less intellectually mature and less experienced, she is less able to appreciate the wrongness of her behavior.

For the subjectivist, however, the wrongness of cruelty is not something that, strictly speaking, *can* be known or appreciated. If there is anything to this purported reason for judging the young child less harshly than the older one, the subjectivist must find a less misleading way to describe it. One proposal might be that it is not the knowledge that cruelty is wrong but the knowledge that cruelty will be punished or frowned upon that is a necessary condition for blameworthiness. But the seven-year-old is likely to know this as well as the seventeen-year-old. Alternatively, the subjectivist might take our different attitudes toward less and more mature agents to indicate that it is a condition of responsibility that an agent have been able sufficiently to internalize the values on the basis of which her actions are to be judged. But what, from the subjectivist's point of view, could justify or even explain this condition? The only idea I can think of is that she try to explain this condition by appealing to the consequences of such a requirement. But aside from the question of whether it is reasonable to suppose that there are beneficial consequences to this requirement, we have seen in Chapter 1 that such an approach to understanding the conditions of responsibility already essentially leaves the traditional concept behind.

From the point of view of a subjectivist, it seems, the traditional concept of responsibility makes no sense, at least insofar as it insists on a difference in responsible status between younger and older children, or for that matter, between animals capable of understanding that certain kinds of behavior carry the threat of punishment and normal human adults.[2]

Again, however, such a conclusion would constitute an objection not to the Reason View's account of responsibility but rather to the concept of responsibility itself. In that case, the Reason View, though failing to establish the coherence of our familiar notion of responsibility, would at least be illuminating in tracing its *in*coherence to its metaethical presuppositions and not, as more familiar positions have suggested, to confused theories of agent-causality.

In fact, however, as I have already mentioned, there seems to me little reason to believe that Conceptual Subjectivism is correct. Rather, the reasons typically offered in support of this position seem to me better reasons for positions either broader or narrower than this one. We have already noted that some of the arguments that lead to skepticism about the objectivity of values seem equally applicable to nonevaluative realms. Thus, the articulation of one's reasons for thinking at first that value judgments are incapable of satisfactory justification or that evaluative beliefs are not properly true or false may reveal implicit models of justification or truth that turn out to be unrealistic and implausible in any context. To that extent, such reflections should lead, not to skepticism about the objectivity of values *per se*, but to skepticism about the notion of objectivity more generally or about the conceptions of reason, justification, and truth that are traditionally associated with this notion. Impressive arguments along these lines have been given recently by many philosophers, among them Donald Davidson, Richard Rorty, Hilary Putnam, John McDowell, and David Wiggins.

Even acknowledging the force of such arguments, however, the subjectivist may insist that differences between evaluative and non-evaluative judgments remain, citing as evidence the pervasiveness of normative disagreements and the difficulty of even conceiving of a means of settling them. This point seems to me to stand up against the familiar objectivist attempts to diffuse it by pointing out the ways in which apparently irresolvable differences may turn out to be resolvable after all, or to depend on different nonevaluative beliefs, or different social conventions, or different concrete circumstances. But here I believe that the conclusions the subjectivist draws are too broad.

The existence of basic disagreements that are not resolvable by Reason leads one to subjectivism only if one takes it as evidence that Reason has nothing to say about values at all. But the issue may not be *whether* Reason has anything to say about values, but *what*. The fact that Reason cannot choose between two particular actions or policies, or even two particular systems of value or normative theories, does not imply that Reason never supports one choice above all others or, as important, that Reason does not constrain the options among which it fails to choose. To put it differently, it does not imply that values cannot be correct or incorrect, or that value judgments can never be fully true. Rather, it may point to the fact that the truth about values, even in conjunction with, say, the truth about human psychology and concrete circumstances, is merely insufficient to determine a single specifiable way of life.

If this is right, then there will be differences between the way we think about the empirical world and the way we ought to think about normative issues that may strike one as unsettling. Thus, when thinking about the empirical world, we know that even if our evidence points equally to each of two inconsistent propositions (some evidence points to the butler's having done it, for example, other evidence to the mother-in-law), at most one or the other of these propositions can be true. But if there are good reasons for one policy, and good reasons for another, there needn't be one or the other that is really better, or right. This is, if you like, a disanalogy between normative claims and empirical ones, but it supports no metaphysical claims about the status of normative claims generally. It does not, for example, support the claim that there is no truth about value. The truth, in this case, may be simply that there are good reasons for each policy (which distinguish them from many other policies) and no non-question-begging reason for preferring one to the other.

Normative Pluralism and Its Conjunction with the Reason View

The view that although Reason constrains values it does not constrain them completely, and that therefore there may be two or more normative positions that are equally and maximally supported by Reason (or, somewhat differently, two or more positions that are both supported by Reason such that there is no non-question-begging reason for preferring one to the other), I shall call

Normative Pluralism. As I suggested earlier, it may be thought to represent a view according to which values are *partially* objective. It is the view that seems by far the most plausible to me, if only because it can accommodate the thought that, while some systems of value are clearly better than others, there are many controversies, within cultures and between cultures, at the level of practice and at the level of theory, that do not appear to have a right answer.

Of course, I do not mean to suggest that every time immediate inspection fails to reveal a right answer to a problem, we should simply assume that there isn't one and that all popular contenders are equally and positively acceptable. Rather, my point is that, however desirable it might be to have a single right answer to every normative question, the supposition that there must be such an answer is no part of a belief in the objectivity of values. Indeed, when we express the belief in the objectivity of values in terms of the thesis that normative judgments are susceptible to evaluation by Reason, there seems no reason whatsoever to expect the supposition of uniqueness to be true. Why should the reasons for and against different actions, policies, ideals, ways of life, and so on converge in such a way as to point to a single optimal choice? What expectations we do have that there will be a single best set of values for everyone must be counted as nonrational ones, resulting, perhaps, from a combination of wish-fulfillment, unjustified presumptions based on features of ordinary language, and a tendency too readily to draw analogies between normative and perceptual and scientific discourse.[3]

To engage in a full elaboration of Normative Pluralism, explaining the various forms it may take and the various levels at which there may be normative pluralities, to work out all the significant implications of this view, while avoiding its evident pitfalls, would be needlessly complicated for present purposes. One feature of this view deserves special mention, however, not only for its contribution to a proper understanding of the view itself but also for its special usefulness when Normative Pluralism is conjoined with the conception of responsibility proposed by the Reason View.

Normative Pluralism is a view about the objectivity of values, a view that I have said may be informally understood as one according to which values and value judgments are partially objective. What I want now to emphasize is that, although contemporary discussions of the objectivity of values typically focus exclusively on *moral* values or systems of value, the view I am advocating is intended as a view about values much more generally. There may be a plurality, not only of good moral outlooks, but also of good aesthetic values and of good personal ideals. (Indeed, if debates about the objectivity of values focused more on these evaluative realms, the option of Normative Pluralism would probably be much more widely recognized, since a position of pluralism with respect to these realms is much closer to common sense.) Equally important, there may be a plurality of good ways to integrate these different types of values, or, to put it differently, a plurality of good ways to integrate the reasons that are generated from these different normative points of view.[4] The view that value judgments are constrained by Reason, then, must be understood broadly enough to encompass the proper influence of *all* the reasons there are. The view that such constraints may be insufficient to yield a wholly determinate system of values must be understood to suggest not only that there may not be a uniquely best moral system but also that there may not be a uniquely right answer to the question of *how* moral to be.

If, in fact, the constraints imposed by Reason leave open a plurality of values and ideals in the ways suggested above, then our image of the agent who is most able to see and understand what reasons there are need not coincide with that of the agent who is most acutely sensitive particularly to *moral* reasons. Appreciation of the Good need not be confined to appreciation of the *moral* Good. Indeed, in certain contexts, appreciation of the moral good may interfere with one's ability to appreciate the nonmoral good or with one's ability to recognize reasons for preferring a morally inferior course of action. Thus, one's disapproval of bigotry may prevent one from enjoying an immoral but funny ethnic joke. One's commitment to impartiality may block one's recognition of reasons that originate in bonds of friendship and love.[5] Just as Reason may fail to pick out a uniquely best conception of impartiality, Reason may fail to select a uniquely best conception of how, and how much, one's conception of impartiality should be reflected in one's life.

If we understand the Reason View against the background of Normative Pluralism, and more particularly against the background of a form of Normative Pluralism that stresses the plurality of ways in which morality can reasonably inform one's personal ideals, a picture of the responsible agent emerges that is somewhat different from the one the Reason View suggests in the absence of that background and that provides us with a basis for answering an important objection to the conception of responsibility proposed by the Reason View. Specifically, it offers an answer to the objection that the Reason View's conception of responsibility conflates an interest in freedom with an interest in goodness, and that being able to act in accordance with the True and the Good, despite its evident desirability, has relatively little to do with the desirability of being free.

To be sure, the objector may say, in contexts of moral heroism and moral turpitude, where issues of praiseworthiness and blame-worthiness are at stake, the ability to understand and act in accordance with the True and the Good may be admitted as a condition of moral responsibility. But our interest in freedom and responsibility generally may be pried apart from these contexts, and when it is, our concern seems to be more about whether we are able to act according to our own lights, so to speak, lights that may coincide with the True and the Good or may not. Being able to act in accordance with true and good values, if one is unable to do anything but that, seems, from this point of view, as bad as any other form of determination. For it seems to imply that one's life is being pushed along a single track off of which one is helpless to jump, and this seems objectionable even after one has acknowledged that there is no other track on which one would rather be, and indeed, no other track on which one *ought* to be.[6]

With this objection, an explicit fear of determinism seems to resurface once again, and this may suggest that the Reason View's attempt to provide an alternative to the standard compatibilist and incompatibilist accounts of freedom and responsibility is just an evasion of the real issue after all. In light of our discussion of Normative Pluralism, however, this objection can be answered or, more precisely, redirected. For further reflection reveals that the power of the objection comes not from the conception of freedom and responsibility encapsulated in the Reason View but from an implausibly narrow and rigid conception of Reason itself.

The objection, remember, is that insofar as we are concerned specifically about freedom and responsibility, our concern is about acting by our own lights, and this may coincide with acting in accordance with the True and the Good or it may not. Of course, most people may also hope that their actions *do* accord with the True and the Good. The point of the objection is to insist that these are different issues.

One respect in which they are different issues can clearly be accommodated within the Reason View. For there is at least a superficial sense in which one's actions can be "in accordance with" the True and the Good that does not imply that the actions are an expression of the agent's values at all. A person who is hypnotized, coerced, or even neurotically driven to satisfy the wishes of an authority figure may, if the authority figure herself happens to have good values, thereby end up performing actions that Reason would independently support. In such a case, the agent is clearly not doing the right thing *for the right reasons*, and so the Reason View would not regard this as any positive indication of the agent's freedom and responsibility.

Acknowledging this, however, the critic may press the objection in a way that does seem problematic for the Reason View. For such examples seem only to support the point that our interest in freedom is an interest in acting according to *our own* reasons, and not, as the Reason View suggests, an interest in acting by *right* reasons. The Reason View's stress on the rightness of reasons thus seems at best irrelevant and at worst contrary to freedom as an ideal (for, it might be thought, if one is too exclusively attentive to right reasons, this may limit one's freedom seriously to entertain wrong ones).

Here, however, our discussion of Normative Pluralism may be brought to bear. For although it is easy to understand and sympathize with this objection when one interprets right reasons to refer dominantly if not exclusively to specifically moral, puritanical, or otherwise narrow or rigid patterns of thought, it becomes less and less intelligible as one acknowledges the rightness or legitimacy of reasons from a larger variety of sources. Thus, it is easy to contrast the ideal of choosing freely (for oneself) with the ideal of choosing rightly if one imagines a situation for which there is, as one thinks, an admittedly right choice but for which there is also a lot to be said for the other side. If understanding and appreciating the right reasons referred only to understanding the reasons *in favor of* the right choice, then one might legitimately complain that a choice exclusively determined by these would be less than fully free. The Reason View, however, associates freedom and responsibility with the ability to understand and appreciate *whatever* reasons there are, and this includes not only the reasons in favor of what may ultimately be the right choice but the reasons against it as well. The point of the Reason View is best understood not in terms of a contrast between the ability to act in accordance with the right reasons and the ability to act in accordance with the wrong, but in terms of a contrast between the ability to act in accordance with Reason and the possibility of not acting by Reason at all. It makes *no* contribution to freedom and responsibility, according to the Reason View, that the agent be able (or free) to act *ir*rationally— that is, at the limit, insanely. It makes *no* contribution, according to the Reason View, that the agent be able *not* to see what reasons there are. But insofar as seeing the world rightly involves seeing reasons for (and against) many different options, then maximum freedom and responsibility would presumably involve being able to see them all.

In fact, against the background of Normative Pluralism, the evidently powerful contrast between the ideal of acting freely and that of acting rightly may actually be used to support the Reason View, which it was initially introduced to criticize. For the power of this contrast may be interpreted as deriving from the insight that even good reasoning, if it is incomplete, and if the ways in which it is incomplete are outside the agent's control, may constitute an insidious and objectionable form of blindness. Although indoctrination into sexism and bigotry is in obvious ways worse than indoctrination into justice and love for humanity, from the point of view of freedom they are equally offensive, for being indoctrinated is, by definition, opposed to being *convinced*—by, for example, a sensitive and careful examination of the issues, a rehearsal of the arguments on both sides, and the exercise of seeing the problem from different relevant points of view.

This perspective on freedom, however, far from being opposed to the Reason View, confirms its fundamental insight. For, while the Reason View acknowledges what any plausible account of freedom and responsibility must acknowledge—that part of freedom and responsibility consists in an individual's ability to govern her behavior in accordance with her deepest values—its originality lies in the claim that the other part of freedom and responsibility lies in the agent's ability to form or revise her deepest values in light of the truth. Thus, it analyzes what fear of determinism remains, after the recognition that determinism is compatible with the ability to govern one's actions by one's values, as the fear that determinism implies a form of blindness to all or part of the truth. In other words, it analyzes what fear of determinism is left as the fear (as it happens, unjustified) that determinism implies that all values are a product of indoctrination, or, perhaps, that the distinction between indoctrination and reasoned conviction cannot be intelligibly applied.

It is understandable that emphasis on certain features of the Reason View should lead to the misunderstanding on which the objection we have been considering is based, a misunderstanding that might be captured by an image according to which it is thought to be all right that one's life is pushed along a single track so long as it is the track that goes along the prettiest stream and passes by the most delicate flowers in the safest possible way. This image fails to reflect the fact that there is something to be said for adventure even when it conflicts with safety, that there is a certain interest in urban and industrial scenes as opposed to pastoral ones, an interest that, according to the Reason View, a maximally free and responsible agent must also have at least the ability to consider. It would seem that one cannot build this into the picture unless one imagines the individual to be charting her own track. Still, if she comes to a fork where a left turn would mean colliding with an oncoming train, the result of which would be her instant death and the horrible disfigurement of many of her friends, then the fact that these considerations *make* her turn right does not compromise her status as a free and responsible agent. To the contrary, it seems only to testify to her competence as a driver.

Since the Reason View connects responsibility with the ability to appreciate *whatever* reasons there are, its conjunction with Normative Pluralism implies that *full* freedom and responsibility will involve the ability to appreciate reasons that come from a variety of sources, not necessarily all commensurable, and not necessarily capable of yielding determinate decisions in every case. Thus, one's freedom and responsibility may be compromised, not only by events that make one take bad values for good ones and wrong reasons for right, but also by an upbringing that leads one, help-lessly, to the mistaken belief that one's values are the *only* good values to have and that one's subsequent choices are the *only* reasonable choices to make. One might plausibly think that many of the values our society tries to instill in us are basically reasonable and sound, but take objection to what seems to be a tendency to discourage open-minded questioning beyond a certain point. Inso-far as initiation into social values prevents one from taking se-riously sensible alternative options, what passes for moral educa-tion might more properly be called social conditioning. The Reason View means to acknowledge this and insists that responsibility involves the ability to appreciate values that are reasonable *period*, not merely reasonable from some socially dominant point of view.

In light of this, worries that the conception of freedom and responsibility advanced by the Reason View is insufficiently atten-tive to the value of having multiple alternatives, a value so promi-nent in our intuitions about freedom, may be put to rest. For, especially if Normative Pluralism is true, the agent who cannot help being governed by Reason will still have plenty of room to move within this constraint. By the same token, however, new worries may arise, for it may be feared that, against the background of Normative Pluralism, the ideal of the free and responsible agent is, though metaphysically possible, intellectually unattainable and per-haps unattractive as well.

How Much Freedom (and Reason) Do We Need?

Once it is emphasized that freedom and responsibility involve the ability to see *whatever* reasons there are, one may begin to wonder how extensive, how deep, and how clear one's vision has to be. If the Reason View is interpreted to imply that the free and responsi-ble agent must be able to recognize and appreciate *all* the values that could arguably be considered relevant to any particular action or choice, it is doubtful that anyone would turn out to be a free and responsible agent. The task of discovering all the reasons for and against every choice we make would require greater powers of reflection and imagination, a greater breadth of knowledge, and a greater amount of leisure time than any of us have. And, even if we did have the time and the intellectual capabilities, it is hard to see how it would be worthwhile to engage in such an extensive survey of considerations. Surely, in reflecting on my temptation to steal vegetables from my neighbor's garden, I do not have to rehearse the Kantian arguments *and* the consequentialist arguments *and* the prudential arguments against it. Indeed, it is not clear that I need rehearse arguments at all in this case. A reflexive disapproval of stealing, given that it has survived years of self-reflection and questioning, seems all that is necessary for a responsible decision here.

What this brings out is that, usually, our interest in freedom and responsibility is an interest in *enough* freedom and responsibility to satisfy the purposes and interests at hand. The range of reasons and values, and the thoroughness of understanding, that the Reason View requires a free and responsible agent to be able to have will correspondingly vary with the context.

In contexts in which the justification of a reactive attitude or an attribution of praise or blame is at stake, we will be particularly interested in the agent's ability to recognize and appreciate a set of reasons sufficient to show which action or choice would be right. That is, if the agent has done something bad or wrong, we will want to know whether she was capable of appreciating that it was wrong and that something else would have been better. If, on the other hand, the agent did something that we are initially inclined to admire, we will want to know whether her doing it involved a sufficient appreciation of what made the action good.

These general remarks are not easy to spell out in detail. There are cases in which an agent is moved by feelings that we regard as praiseworthy but that the agent herself is incapable of appreciating in that light (for example, the famous case of Huckleberry Finn's decision not to turn in Jim), and there are cases in which our admiration for an agent actually depends on that agent's not thinking of her behavior as deserving of praise.[7] Even in straightforward cases, it is hard to specify what counts as sufficient ability to appreciate reasons and values, for one wants to give an account that will make the point that rote acceptance of and habituation to the values of one's parents or one's church does not constitute appreciation of these values without at the same time overrating the importance of the role of articulate, intellectual moral reflection and introspection.

When the question of an agent's freedom and responsibility is raised independently of contexts of praise and blame, what can be said about the acceptable scope of an agent's ability to appreciate right reasons and good values is even more vague. Roughly, it seems that the greater the range of reasons and values one is in a position to appreciate, the more free one is. The more options and the more reasons for them that one is capable of seeing and understanding, the more fully one can claim one's choice to be one's own. But it is important to keep in mind that, beyond a certain point, the value of fuller freedom and responsibility may be quite small, and the realization that one's inability to appreciate some foreign or esoteric values limits one's freedom of the will need be no more upsetting than the realization that one's inability to flap one's wings and fly or to eat a pair of cufflinks limits one's freedom of action. Indeed, a possible drawback to appreciating more reasons and values rather than less is that this may reveal a plurality of (equally or incommensurably) reasonable options, whereas a less extensive survey of reasons might have suggested only one. Though the ability to appreciate more values and more options may give one an increase in freedom, the value of that increase may be outweighed by the disvalue of the added difficulty of decisionmaking that accompanies it.[8]

Thus, although the Reason View, like any theory that purports to analyze freedom and responsibility, implicitly contains a conception of what the maximally free and responsible agent is like, it does not thereby assume that maximum freedom and responsibility comprise a rational, much less a uniquely rational, ideal. Still, insofar as understanding a theory's maximal realization can illuminate the theory, it will be useful to make one further point about the Reason View's conception of a maximally free and responsible agent. Since the point of the Reason View is to stress that the kind of freedom we need for responsibility is a freedom within Reason, a freedom to be governed by Reason (or, if you like, Rationally to govern ourselves), it may be thought that, insofar as Reason fails to pick out a uniquely best choice, the maximally free agent must be able to choose among the Rationally acceptable choices independently of all forces whatsoever. Such an understanding, however, seems to me to be a symptom of a continued tendency to see freedom and responsibility as ultimately metaphysical matters, and not, as the Reason View proposes, as more primarily normative ones.

According to the Reason View, one's freedom and responsibility are diminished insofar as one's values and choices are determined by things that interfere with or prevent the exercise of one's ability to appreciate and act in accordance with the True and the Good. If, however, one's decision is determined by factors that do not block the efficacy of right reason—if, for example, the determination by these factors is itself conditioned by their rational acceptability— then the agent's responsibility is in no way impaired. Indeed, if reasons cannot, on logical grounds, provide a basis for choosing one option rather than the other, then a choice that is independent of nonrational grounds is simply a random choice. This seems to be a case in which the familiar point that randomness is no better, from the point of view of an agent's control, than nonrational determination should lead us to conclude that a choice among equally rational options that is determined by nonrational factors is as free and responsible as a choice among rational options that is not determined at all. If, moreover, the nonrational factors that determine one's choice in such a situation are ones with which an agent deeply identifies—if, for example, one's choice among rational options is explained by one's distinctly female perspective or one's philosophical tendencies, or by one's love of music or sports— then one can embrace that choice as a fuller (though not a more responsible) expression of one's deep self than it would be if one's choice were not determined at all. (This remark should not be taken to suggest that these sorts of character traits are not relevant to what counts as rational for the agent as well.)

Admittedly, however, factors of the sort just mentioned may also contribute to the determination of one's decisions in ways that are not compatible with maximum responsibility. Certain sorts of religious perspectives, for instance, may not only give one the basis of a decision in cases of a rational tie but may also keep one from seeing that there is a rational tie, or even prevent one from recognizing an option that is more rational than any one is considering. According to the Reason View, one's responsibility is diminished insofar as one is, as in the last case, prevented from recognizing what is best. How important it is to be free of such influences will, as was earlier suggested, vary according to the context.

Sometimes it is reasonable to be concerned that some aspects of oneself, even aspects that one cherishes, might prevent one from recognizing alternative but equally worthy values. Strictly speaking, one has more freedom, in the sense that gives one greater control of one's life, insofar as one is capable of appreciating a greater range of options and reasons. One is responsible for the choices one makes relative to the options that one could have reasonably assessed, but one is not responsible for those choices relative to a larger set that includes options one was incapable of understanding at the time. Nonetheless, in most contexts we are, and ought to be, satisfied with less than the maximum ability to choose.

If inevitable features of myself—my gender, my race, my nationality, for example—and rationally arbitrary choices and twists of fate have shaped my values and decisions, this does not seem to me to place objectionable limits on my status as a free and responsible agent. As long as these nonrational determinants do not prevent me from a sufficiently open-minded and clear-headed assessment of my values to allow me to see whether they fall into the range of the reasonable, and as long as my blindness to some other reasonable alternatives does not lead me to acts of intolerance or prejudice, then it seems that, for most intents and purposes, I am free and responsible enough. These nonrational determinants are, after all, what give us our individuality and distinctiveness. If, at the limits, they can be in tension with our freedom and responsibility, in more central cases they provide the basis for a substantive identity and an attachment to the world without which no interest in freedom and responsibility could arise.

It would be nice if there were a method for determining how much and what kinds of influences on our characters and values were consistent with right reason—if, for example, one could see whether and in what respects American culture, a Jewish upbringing, a training in economics, allowed or even promoted our abilities to see and understand the world, and in what respects such influences tended instead to distort our perceptions or blunt our reasoning. There is no such method, and so there is always the risk that aspects of our identities limit our status as free and responsible beings in ways we are helpless to discern and so equally helpless to remove. This risk is inevitable, not only because we could not rid ourselves of all influences that were potentially in conflict with Reason if we wanted to, but because we cannot even form a conception of Reason independently of these influences, and it is highly unlikely that, if we tried, what we took to be Reason, by contrast to which other influences were to be judged as nonrational, would really be that.

We are not, then, and never can be fully responsible for whether and how much we *are* responsible. On the other hand, if the Reason View is right, then at least we can see a way to try to enlarge our sphere of freedom and responsibility, and we can see how to raise our children in ways that will tend to promote these qualities in them. In particular, if the Reason View is right, then it is especially important to cultivate and promote an open and active mind and an attitude of alertness and sensitivity to the world. For these are essential features of the ability to appreciate the True and the Good, and so are essential to the ability to form one's values, and direct one's actions, in light of them.

Notes

Chapter 1

1. In this respect, the problem of responsibility is analogous to the problem of skepticism. See Thomas Nagel, "Moral Luck," in Thomas Nagel, *Mortal Questions* (Cambridge: Cambridge University Press, 1979), pp. 24–38.

2. See particularly Immanuel Kant, *Foundations of the Metaphysics of Morals*, first edition (1785), trans. and intro. Lewis White Beck (Indianapolis: Bobbs-Merrill, 1975): Second Section p. 59 ff.

3. Some philosophers believe that if we have free will at all, we have it only rarely in exceptional situations. See, for example, C. A. Campbell, "Is 'Freewill' a Pseudo-Problem?" *Mind* 60, no. 240 (October 1951): 446–65.

4. This point is made forcefully in David Wiggins, "Towards a Reasonable Libertarianism," in T. Honderich, ed., *Essays on Freedom of Action* (London: Routledge & Kegan Paul, 1973).

5. Moritz Schlick, "When Is a Man Responsible?" in *Problems of Ethics*, trans. David Rynins (New York: Prentice-Hall, 1939), pp. 143–56.

6. For a brilliant presentation of this view, see P. F. Strawson, "Freedom and Resentment," Proceedings of the British Academy, 48 (1962) pp. 1–25.

7. I argue for the claims of these last two sections in a very different way in "The Importance of Free Will," *Mind* 90 (July 1981): 385–405.

149

Chapter 2

1. David Hume, *A Treatise Concerning Human Nature*, (1888), ed. L. A. Selby-Bigge (Oxford: Oxford University Press, 1967), p. 407.

2. Some philosophers of mind might object that this characterization is redundant, for there is at least one very broad sense of "desire" according to which it is tautological that if an agent willed, or intended, to do something, she must have wanted, or desired, to do it. But because, as we shall see, the question of which desires shape the content of the agent's will is important to a more satisfactory model of normally free action, it is useful to distinguish the will from the set of desires from the start.

3. This analysis derives from Harry Frankfurt, "Freedom of the Will and the Concept of a Person," *Journal of Philosophy* 68 (January 1971): 5–20.

4. Gary Watson, "Free Agency," *Journal of Philosophy* 72 (April 1975): 205–20.

5. This should be qualified, since the coercion example, as I have so sketchily described it, might plausibly be interpreted in either of two ways. On the one hand, we may interpret it in the way I have above as a case in which, given the strength of the agent's desire, his circumstances compel him to act as the coercer demands, independently of whether he judges it permissible or right. In that case, the agent is not responsible for what he does. On the other hand, it may be interpreted as a case in which the agent's behavior is not literally compelled, but is rather dependent on his judgment that, given his circumstances, obeying the coercer's wishes is reasonable. In that case, the agent is responsible for what he does, though not—at least if we agree with his judgment—blameworthy for it.

6. R. E. Hobart, "Free Will as Involving Determination and Inconceivable Without It," in Bernard Berofsky, ed., *Free Will and Determinism* (New York: Harper & Row 1966), p. 83.

7. This and related suggestions are discussed further in Susan Wolf, "Sanity and the Metaphysics of Responsibility," in Ferdinand Schoeman, ed., *Responsibility, Character, and the Emotions* (Cambridge: Cambridge University Press, 1987), pp. 46–62.

Chapter 3

1. See C. A. Campbell, "Is 'Freewill' a Pseudo-Problem? *Mind* 60, no. 240 (October 1951): 446–65.

2. Jean-Paul Sartre, "Existentialism Is a Humanism," in W. Kaufmann, ed. *Existentialism from Dostoevsky to Sartre* (New York: New America Library, 1975), pp. 345–69.

Chapter 4

1. I have in mind the possibility that in extreme cases, involving, for example, self-destructiveness or extraordinary evil, the ability to act in discord once with Reason may indicate some form of insanity.

2. This way of putting it is misleading insofar as it implicitly suggests that there will always be a *single* uniquely rational option. For stylistic purposes, I shall talk in this chapter of "the" option to act in accordance with Reason, but it should be understood that when I say that someone has that option, I mean that she has *at least* one option to act in accordance with Reason and that she has that option because she recognizes it (at least) to be in accordance with Reason.

3. I have in mind the notion of immanent causation, also known as agent-causality, discussed, for example, by Roderick Chisholm.

4. The term is taken from Robert Nozick, *Philosophical Explanations* (Cambridge: Harvard University Press, 1981).

5. This point might also be made in terms of the Reason View's analysis of the phrase "he could have done otherwise" when that phrase is used to express the condition of freedom required for responsibility. For more on this see my "Asymmetrical Freedom," *Journal of Philosophy* 77 (March 1980): 151–66. (Portions of this chapter are from that article.)

6. The question of whether a belief in neurophysiological or, for that matter, divine determinism might constitute a reason will be discussed in Chapter 5.

7. I here leave aside questions about people who cannot help doing the wrong thing at the time of performance, but who could have kept themselves from getting into that position at some earlier time.

8. This is the suggestion of Harry Frankfurt in "Freedom of the Will and the Concept of a Person," *Journal of Philosophy* 68 (January 1971): 5–20.

Chapter 5

1. J. L. Austin, "Ifs and Cans," in Austin, *Philosophical Papers* (Oxford: Oxford University Press, 1970), p. 218.

2. This line of argument might be used as part of a response to the Ginet/Van Inwagen argument for incompatibilism, forcefully presented in Peter Van Inwagen, *An Essay on Free Will* (Oxford: Oxford University Press, 1983). For, in attempting to establish that determinism implies that it is not in anyone's power to do anything other than what she actually did, the Ginet/Van Inwagen argument relies on the premise that it is not in anyone's power to affect the laws of nature or any state of the world existing prior to one's birth. Curiously, there is a sense in which the persons

in the story might be said to have the power (by way of God's foreknowledge and interests) to affect the laws of nature or states of the world prior to their birth. Thus, one might argue that the Ginet/Van Inwagen argument does not apply to the persons in the story. If this were admitted, however, along with the conclusion that these persons were free though determined, it would throw doubt on the strength of the argument even in our own case. If the psychological abilities possessed by the people in the story are sufficient for their freedom and responsibility, why wouldn't those same abilities be sufficient for us?

3. More formally, this means that they are faced with choices for which it is compatible with their psychological histories up to the point of these choices, in conjunction with all the psychological and psychophysical laws that are true of them, that they choose one way, and it is also compatible with all this that they choose another.

4. Some evidence for this suspicion can be found in Norman Malcolm, "The Conceivability of Mechanism," *Philosophical Review* 77 (January 1968): 133.

Chapter 6

1. A nonnormative fact, rather than a normative fact, because it supports no particular policy, action, or attitude, not even a policy or attitude of tolerance.

2. Similarly, there seems a difference in status between sociopaths and normal human adults. I refer to this as the difference between practical and moral responsibility in "The Legal and Moral Responsibility of Organizations," in J. Roland Pennock and John W. Chapman, eds., *Criminal Justice: Nomos 27* (New York: New York University Press, 1985).

3. This outlook is in many respects similar to, and undoubtedly influenced by, that of Bernard Williams in *Ethics and the Limits of Philosophy* (Cambridge, Mass.: Harvard University Press, 1985). However, while Williams stresses the distance between his view and more traditional objectivist positions, I want to stress the degree to which this outlook is consistent with fundamental objectivist claims. See my review of Williams's book in *Ethics* 97 (July 1987): 821–33.

4. See my "Moral Saints," *Journal of Philosophy* 79 (August 1982): 419–39.

5. For other examples, see my "Above and Below the Line of Duty," *Philosophical Topics 14* (Fall 1986): 131–48.

6. An objection of this sort is suggested in Paul Benson, "Freedom and Value," *Journal of Philosophy* 84 (September 1987).

7. See Julia Driver, "Virtues of Ignorance," *Journal of Philosophy* 86 (July 1989). 373–84.

8. See Gerald Dworkin, "Is More Choice Better than Less?" in Gerald Dworkin, *The Theory and Practice of Autonomy* (Cambridge: Cambridge University Press, 1988), pp. 62–81.

Selected Readings

Collections and Anthologies

Berofsky, Bernard, ed., *Free Will and Determinism* (New York: Harper & Row, 1966).

Fischer, John Martin, ed., *Moral Responsibility* (Ithaca: Cornell University Press, 1986.))

Honderich, Ted, ed., *Essays on Freedom of Action* (London: Routledge & Kegan Paul, 1973).

Lehrer, Keith, ed., *Freedom and Determinism* (New York: Random House, 1966).

Schoeman, Ferdinand, *Responsibility, Character, and the Emotions* (Cambridge: Cambridge University Press, 1987).

Watson, Gary, ed., *Free Will* (Oxford: Oxford University Press, 1982).

Books and Articles

Chisholm, Roderick, "Freedom and Action," in Lehrer (1966). Reprinted in part as "Human Freedom and the Self" in Watson (1982).

Dennett, Daniel, "Mechanism and Responsibility," in Honderich (1973). Reprinted in Watson (1982).

————*Elbow Room: Varieties of Free Will Worth Wanting* (Cambridge, Mass.: MIT Press, 1984).

Duggan, Timothy, and Gert, Bernard, "Free Will as the Ability to Will" *Nous* 13 (May 1979) 197–217. Reprinted in Fischer (1986).

Dworkin, Gerald, *The Theory and Practice of Autonomy* (Cambridge: Cambridge University Press, 1988).

Farrer, Austin, *The Freedom of the Will* (London: Adam & Charles Black, 1958).

Frankfurt, Harry, "Alternate Possibilities and Moral Responsibility," *Journal of Philosophy* 66 (December 1969) 828–39. Reprinted in Fischer (1986).

————"Freedom of the Will and the Concept of a Person," *Journal of Philosophy* 68 (January 1971) 5–20. Reprinted in Watson (1982) and Fischer (1986).

Hampshire, Stuart, *Freedom of the Individual* (Princeton: Princeton University Press, 1975).

Malcolm, Norman, "The Conceivability of Mechanism," *Philosophical Review* 77 (January 1968) 45–72. Reprinted in Watson (1982).

Murdoch, Iris, *The Sovereignty of Good* (London: Routledge & Kegan Paul, 1970).

Strawson, Galen, *Freedom and Belief* (Oxford: Oxford University Press, 1986).

Strawson, P. F., "Freedom and Resentment," *Proceedings of the British Academy* 48, pp. 1–25. Repinted in Watson (1982).

Nagel, Thomas, "Moral Luck," in Nagel, *Mortal Questions* (Cambridge: Cambridge University Press, 1979). Reprinted in Watson (1982).

————*The View From Nowhere* (New York: Oxford University Press, 1986).

Taylor, Charles, "Responsibility for Self," in Rorty, ed., *The Identities of Persons* (Berkeley: University of California Press, 1976). Reprinted in Watson (1982).

Taylor, Richard, *Metaphysics* (Englewood Cliffs: Prentice-Hall, 1963).

Van Inwagen, Peter, *An Essay on Free Will* (Oxford: Oxford University Press, 1986).

Watson, Gary, "Free Agency," *Journal of Philosophy* 72 (April 1975) 205–20. Reprinted in Watson (1982) and Fischer (1986).

————"Free Action and Free Will," *Mind* 96 (1987) 145–72.

Wiggins, David "Towards a Reasonable Libertarianism" in Honderich (1973).

Wolf, Susan, "Asymmetrical Freedom," *Journal of Philosophy* 77 (March 1980) 151–66. Reprinted in Fischer (1986).

———"The Importance of Free Will," *Mind* 90 (July 1981) 386–405.
———"The Legal and Moral Responsibility of Organizations" in J. R. Pennock and J. W. Chapman, eds. *Criminal Justice: Nomos* 27 (New York: New York University Press, 1985).
———"Sanity and the Metaphysics of Responsibility" in Schoeman (1987).

Index